SPALDING®

Youth

HOCKEY

For Parents and Players

GERALD A. WALFORD, PH.D
& GERALD E. WALFORD

MASTERS PRESS
SPORTS PUBLISHER

A Division of Howard W. Sams & Co.

D1198456

Published by Masters Press
(A Division of Howard W. Sams)
2647 Waterfront Pkwy. E. Dr., Suite 300
Indianapolis, IN 46214

© 1994 Gerald A. Walford

Printed in the United States of America

Library of Congress Cataloging-in-Publication Data

Walford, Gerald A., 1941 –
    Youth hockey: for parents and players/ Gerald A. Walford and Gerald E. Walford.
          p.   cm.
     ISBN 0-940279-89-4 : $12.95
     1. Hockey for children. 2. Hockey for children --Coaching.
I. Walford, Gerald E., 1963 –   . II. Title
GV848.6.C45W35   1993   93-47568
  796.962'07'7--dc 20   CIP

Credits:

Cover photos © Frank Howard, Protography
Cover design by Julie Biddle
Edited by H.W. Kondras and Jon Glesing
Diagrams by Julie Biddle and Lisa Barnett

Contents

The Better Sports for Kids Program

The Better Sports for Kids program is the proud mission of the National Youth Sports Coaches Association (NYSCA) which was created in 1981 to help improve out-of-school sports for over 20 million young people under the age of 16.

The nonprofit association's staff of professionals work to implement a variety of programs, all in cooperation with national, state, and local associations.

The Better Sports for Kids program and its wide range of services help parents and kids get the most out of their participation in youth sports through programs such as the National Youth Sports Coaches Association national certification program coaches, the National Association of Youth Leagues which helps leagues with all their needs in running a youth league organization, the All-American Drug-Free Team program which joins coaches and players in a drug education and prevention program, and the early introduction to lifetime sports through programs such as Hook a Kid on Golf.

The NYSCA is pleased to endorse the Spalding Youth League Series as an informative selection of coaching materials for youth coaches who wish to provide quality instruction and promote self esteem on and off the playing field.

I. Skating

Skating is the basis of hockey. Good players are good skaters. If you want to be a good hockey player, you must practice all phases of skating: the basic stride, the quick breaks, turns, stop and go, and backward. Proper skating technique will improve your speed, power and agility.

Skating and Running - A Comparison

The biggest problem youngsters have when learning to skate is that they try to skate as if they were running. The skills of running and skating are extremely different. If one knows the difference between running and skating, it is much easier to teach or learn correct skating technique.

When walking or running, the runner's leg moves forward and the foot strikes the ground under the body (diagram 1). The leg then continues to push straight back toward the direction of travel. The legs move straight forward and straight back in line with the direction of travel. This is shown in diagram 1.

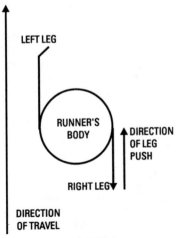

Diagram 1-1

1

Now, look at diagram 2. Notice the leg action of the skater. The skater's leg moves under the body for the glide and then pushes to the side, not backwards like the runner. The leg will actually move in a circle to its maximum extension when it is lifted off the ice and returned to the ice under the body for the glide.

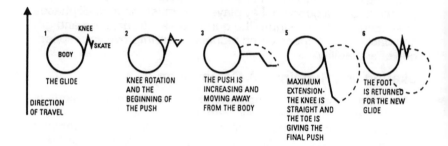

| THE GLIDE | KNEE ROTATION AND THE BEGINNING OF THE PUSH | THE PUSH IS INCREASING AND MOVING AWAY FROM THE BODY | MAXIMUM EXTENSION- THE KNEE IS STRAIGHT AND THE TOE IS GIVING THE FINAL PUSH | THE FOOT IS RETURNED FOR THE NEW GLIDE |

DIRECTION OF TRAVEL

Diagram 1-2

When the legs make this circle it is important to let the knee rotate outward with the leg. Beginners and poor skaters do not rotate the leg outward in a circular pattern. They make the mistake of pushing the leg straight back as in running and then rotating the ankle so that the blade of the skate digs into the ice for the thrust. If the whole leg is rotated outward in a circular pattern, with the knee leading, the skate blade will also be rotated into the required position for maximum thrust and power.

The shoulder action of the runner and skater is also different. When running, the action of the runner's shoulders is opposite to the leg action. If the right leg is striding forward, the left arm is swinging forward. The skater's shoulder action is the same as the leg action. If the right leg is gliding forward, the right shoulder and arm are forward.

Forward Skating

THE HEAD AND NECK

The head must maintain an upright position when skating with proper technique, but it also ensures that the player is able to look around for the action and play. While skating forward, the head should maintain the same distance from the ice surface. If you watch a good skater from the side, you will notice that the head will flow along a line level to the ice and will remain at this level as long as the speed is the same despite the bending and straightening of the skater's knees. The neck reacts with the head and keeps the head in line with the spine.

The center of gravity is the balance point of the body. In most cases the center of gravity or the balance point will be slightly below the belly button region. Look at diagram 3 of a skater in full stride. With the leg extended back for the full stride and the body leaning forward for balance, the center of gravity is about half way between the belly button and the spine. This spot is marked with an 'X'. As you skate, the center of gravity will move forward in a straight line level with the ice. Like the head, the center of gravity and head move forward with no bobbing, dipping, lifting or shifting from side to side.

Diagram 1-3

THE SHOULDERS AND ARMS

The arm and shoulder movement should not be excessive. When the skater is not involved with puck control, the arms and shoulders may move more than usual with a shoulder and arm action that rotates around the spine. Quick shoulder movement is often used for quick breaks. If you are taking the quick break while controlling the puck, your shoulder and arm movement will naturally be limited or even eliminated for better puck control.

THE UPPER BODY

Body lean is determined by speed and/or acceleration. As speed increases, body lean also increases. The skater's leg thrust must be directed through the entire body. In diagram 3, you will notice that the extended leg is thrusting or pushing forward through the entire body and through the center of gravity. Maximum speed forward is gained when the pushing action of the legs is directed through the center of gravity. This can be demonstrated by pushing a fellow player down the ice. If you push the player at the shoulders, you will notice how difficult it is to get maximum results. Now push the skater with your hands on his hips (near his balance point) and, you will notice how much easier it is.

Upper body lean should never be more than 45 degrees because the body will be off-balance if the thrust is directed over the center of gravity and over the head. The upper body should not sway or shift from side to side. If you watch a good skater skate straight towards you, you will notice how the upper body, especially the chest area stays facing you as well as in line with you.

THE HIPS

The hips, along with the thighs, provide power and speed to the skating action. The hips will have a little more rotation during the skating stride than the upper body. This is a natural reaction from the action of the legs as strong hips and thighs are required for power. Many hockey players are using weight training to increase the strength of these muscles. Some players are also doing flexibility exercises for better movement and rotation in the hip and leg areas.

THE LEGS

Each skate leg performs three phases. They are:

1. The recovery phase – after the leg makes its final thrust or push, the skate breaks contact with the ice. The skate is lifted off the ice, brought under the body, and placed on the ice for the glide.

2. The gliding phase – occurs when the skate blade retouches the ice and glides while supporting the body.

3. The thrusting or pushing phase – is the power phase of rotating your leg outward to provide the thrusting action of the skating stride.

The following chart shows the movement of each leg in relationship to the other leg.

While the left leg is:	the right leg is:
gliding	pushing
pushing	recovering
pushing (final)	gliding
recovering	pushing (beginning)
gliding	pushing
pushing	recovering

In the gliding phase, your skate is pointed in the direction of travel and supports most of the body's weight. The gliding skate balances the body. The center of gravity shifts over to your gliding leg. From the gliding phase, the knee begins to rotate outward while thrusting into the ice. As the knee continues to rotate outward in a circular pattern, the push becomes stronger and more powerful. As the leg reaches its maximum thrust position with the leg almost straight, the knee rotates inward and pulls the skate into position for the glide.

When the skate is in the gliding phase, good knee bend is essential. Good knee bend will put the leg in correct position for a strong push in the thrusting phase. If the gliding leg has little knee bend, the skater will be unable to get maximum push to the skating stride. With poor or little knee bend, the skater is very erect and in poor balance. You will notice that during the beginning stages of the push, the push is directed sideways. As the leg continues into the later stages of the push, the circular action of the leg will bring the push around more towards the direction of travel. The final push with the toe will be straight ahead. The thrusting phase will start with the leg well bent and continue until the final thrust where the leg is almost straight. Power is achieved by straightening the leg while the leg's skate blade is digging into the ice. The faster and more powerful the thrusting leg can be straightened, the faster and more powerful the skating action.

To execute good knee bend, the skater must also have good ankle bend or flexion. Diagram 4 illustrates this flexion. This ankle flexion is when the toes move toward the knee. Try and bend your knees without bending your ankles, and you will notice how your rear end sticks out behind you. This puts you in an unbalanced position.

Knee Bend (flexion)

Ankle Bend (flexion)

Diagram 1-4

Skates that do not fit properly or are not broken-in will give the skater great difficulty in flexing the ankles. New skates are often stiff and fail to give the skater proper ankle flexion. This causes the leg to hurt as the skate digs into the leg at the top lace area. If a skater is having difficulty flexing the ankle then it may be advantageous to not tie the top one or two laces.

Another problem that results from insufficient ankle flexion and knee bend is a stiff-legged skating stride with very erect posture. A stiff-legged stride means that you are unable to get maximum thrust or push as there is very little straightening of the leg. If your knee cannot rotate outward for the thrust, your skating action will be more like the running action. Since the leg is not rotating outward for maximum thrust, the knee remains pointing straight ahead and the ankle will twist to the side to give some pushing action and a running type of stride.

Another important point in the leg action of the skating stride is to not let the thrusting leg "lock" into the straight-leg position for the final thrust. Releasing from this "locked" position is time consuming, jerky and inefficient.

Backward Skating

Backward skating is essential for defensemen. Modern strategy has the forwards often switching with the defensemen so skating backward becomes a necessary skill for them as well. It is helpful to the team when the forwards can successfully take the defensemen's role to nullify the opposition's attack.

THE HEAD AND NECK

The head and neck must remain in an upright position so that you have good visibility in all directions. If the head droops the skater will have difficulty looking over his shoulder to check his goaltender and his position in relationship to the developing play. If the head is drooped forward, the skater must throw his shoulder back and lift his head to peek backwards. This throwing back of the shoulder can throw the body off-balance or even give a split-second delay to the skater's actions. Keep it simple. Keep your head up and just rotate your head from side to side.

THE ARMS, SHOULDERS AND UPPER BODY

The carriage of the arms, shoulders and upper body is similar to that described in the forward skating section. Weak backward skaters have a tendency to use excessive arm swing and shoulder movement to help build momentum and speed to the skating stride. Young hockey players must not let themselves fall into this habit. Speed and power are achieved through the hips and legs. Learn to use them correctly.

THE HIPS AND LEGS

Your hips must be strong and flexible to help your leg action. A lack of hip flexibility will cause a skater to attempt building up speed through the use of excessive body rotation, twisting or swaying from side to side. If you sway from side to side, you are not skating straight back. Instead you are using a series of diagonal movements similar to a sailboat tacking into the wind. An attacking forward will have a great advantage in getting around a defenseman that is swaying from side-to-side while skating backwards. The forward just makes his move as the backward skater is swaying away from the attacker.

The key to the thrust in backward skating is to develop good inward rotation of the thrusting leg. Remember not to just rotate the ankle because this gives little power to the thrust. The knee must be rotated inward to lead the skate into the thrusting position. In this position, the leg is well bent. From this bent position, the leg is straightened by a powerful extension of the leg. The thrust will be as close to straight back as possible.

Good backward skaters will execute a little arc with their skate blade. Weak backward skaters will execute a large and long arc because of their excessive body sway. Young players must learn to drive the legs powerfully backwards so that the body can move straight back with no sideward action. Good backward skaters are able to lift their skate off the ice after the thrust and place the skate down on the ice for the glide. Weak backward skaters are unable to lift their skates after the thrust because of their body sway. Being able to lift the skate off the ice and place it down for the glide makes it easier for you to maintain your straight line backwards. Also, it is faster leg action and a more efficient skating stride.

Many skaters will skate forward to build up speed, then pivot to backward skating. The reason for doing this is poor backward skating skill. Such skaters are unable to build up speed from a backward start. Under game conditions a defenseman will often be taken out of the play by pivoting to build up speed and pivoting to backward skating. To start backwards from a backward position one must learn to make the first few stride in a powerful manner. The knees must be well-bent and take a powerful thrust with each leg. Do not build up momentum for the backward stride by swaying the body from side to side. To be a good backward skater it is essential to learn to skate backwards from a backward position start and still be able to reach maximum speed quickly.

Backward skating requires practice, lots of it. Young hockey players must learn these skill as soon as possible. As the youngsters become older, the incorrect habits learned at youth are difficult and often impossible to break in later years. The pivot is another example of learning the correct technique when young. The correct pivot can be difficult, but it must be learned. The benefits of learning the correct skill execution becomes more evident every year as the youngster gets older and the competition becomes stronger.

The Pivot

Hockey players must learn to pivot from backward to forward skating and from forward to backward skating. Many skaters pivot by simply twisting the body. This twisting action of the body also results in the skate blades just twisting on the ice. This is a dangerous method for pivoting. A slight imperfection on the ice surface and the skate blade can catch the ice imperfection and throw the skater off balance. To execute a correct pivot, a skater must learn to lift the skate off the ice, pivot the body and replace the skate to the ice in the new direction. The skates must not twist on the ice.

THE BACKWARD TO FORWARD PIVOT

In diagram 5, notice how the skater pivots from backward skating to forward skating without crossing the legs. The amount of turn is simply controlled by the amount of body and leg rotation. Notice in diagram 5 how the skater's left leg is lifted off the ice as the body rotates. The body rotates to the amount of desired turn. When the body is rotated to the desired direction then the skate is placed on the ice to glide in the new direction. From the glide, the leg takes a strong push to increase or maintain speed.

| *Backward skating* | *Left leg lifts off the ice and rotates with the body to face the attacker. The right leg thrusts to the new direction.* | *Body is rotated; left leg is on the ice and glides while right leg takes final thrust.* | *Left leg is now thrusting in new direction as right leg comes around for it's glide.* |

Diagram 1-5

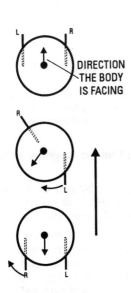

Diagram 1-6

Diagram 1-6 shows the backward to forward pivot from a top view. The right leg is rotated outward while the body rotates in the new direction. This pivot is especially effective when skating backward and facing the puck carrier. In this situation, it is easy to move to either side and continue facing the attacker. If the attacker cuts to the defender's left, then the defender lifts his left leg and rotates his body to the left. If the attacker cuts to the defender's right, the defender simply lifts his right leg, rotates his body to the right and places his skate in the new direction.

An advantage of this type of pivot is that if the attacker gives the defender a quick change of direction, the defender can easily adjust to the attacker's new direction. If during the pivot the defender lifts his left leg off the ice and starts to rotate his body and the attacker changes his cut to the other side, the defender can easily adjust by placing his left leg back on the ice, lifting the right leg and rotating his body to the new direction. When the right leg is placed on the ice, the defender can give a good push in the new direction of travel. Balance is extremely important to executing this skill.

THE FORWARD TO BACKWARD PIVOT

The forward to backward pivot can be a little more difficult. Again there is no crossover action of the legs. The skill is a "pigeon toed" action. To pivot to the left while skating forward, glide on the left leg and body pivot to the left. The right skate is lifted off the ice and "toed inward" to face the toe of the other skate and then placed on the ice to glide backward (diagram 1-7).

The Crossover

The crossover is when the skater crosses one leg over in front of the other leg to turn or cut in a new direction. The skater leans in the direction of the turn, and the inside leg moves under the body. The outside leg crosses over in front of the inside leg for a thrust in the new direction. Often this crossover action takes several crossovers to complete the turn. The

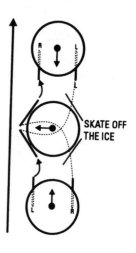

Diagram 1-7

crossover skill is often used to build power to the stride, and it is acceptable in open ice with no agility required by the skater. If the skater is checking someone or requires quick agility moves, the crossover is not a good idea.

There are many reasons for eliminating the crossover action of the legs. Here are some of the reasons.

1. The crossover method does not have the stability of the non-crossover method as the leg crossing over the body is in a weak position and the player can be easily knocked over.

2. Once the leg is crossing over, the skater is committed to the pivot and must complete the pivot before he can readjust. A smart attacker can gain an advantage in getting around a defender committed to his pivot. A quick change of direction by the attacker will often leave the defender out of position.

3. When crossing over, the skater raises his body and straightens his inside leg. Since the outside leg is off the ice and crossing over, the skater is in a non-agile or flatfooted position. The skater cannot get agile or gain power until his outside leg is on the ice and bent for the thrusting action in the new direction. Very often the crossover action puts the skater in a "second-too-late" position.

4. While one leg is off the ice and crossing over, the other leg is twisting on the ice surface for the new direction of travel. This is dangerous as the twisting skate blade can easily catch an imperfection on the ice and throw the skater off-balance and/ or trip him.

These four reasons should be enough to make you learn the correct methods of pivoting and crossing over. It takes practice, but the better players do it.

Stops and Starts in a New Direction

To stop, you must put your skate blades at right angles to your direction of travel. Whenever possible use both blades. One blade can be used but the stop is usually not as quick or as powerful. Also, the one-legged stop is more demanding on the body. The key to a quick stop is to initiate the stop with a quick rotation of the hips, thighs and knees. The lower legs and skates will follow the action of your hips. Beginners and poor skaters will initiate the stop by twisting their skates for the stopping action and then letting their upper body follow the action of their skates. Do not do this. The quicker the hips are rotated, the quicker and more efficient the stop.

When making the stop, the skater must let the knees and ankles bend into a strong flexed position. This flexion gives you a good cushion to the impact of stopping, and it puts the body into position for an explosive start in the new direction. In diagram 8, notice how the inside leg, the left leg in the diagram, lifts off the ice. The knee of the left leg rotates outward towards the new direction of travel. The right leg, which is well bent, is able to achieve a strong thrust by straightening the leg. The left leg is gliding in the new direction while the right leg moves around for it's turn to thrust. This action is similar to the backward skating to forward skating pivot.

| *Two legged stop; right leg is bent* | *Left leg lifts off the ice and rotates to the new direction.* | *Left leg is placed on the ice to glide as right leg is almost fully extended.* | *Left leg glide is now thrusting while right leg moves for a thrust.* |

Diagram 1-8

The key to this skill is to not use the crossover style. At no time will your skate blade twist on the ice. Your outside leg is well-bent and ready for the thrust in the new direction of travel. If the outside leg remains straight, there can be no push with this leg in the new direction. The poor skater has to cross the leg over the inside leg to get into position for a thrust in the new direction. Naturally this action causes a delay in the change of directions. We all know how ineffective this can be. Remember to bend both legs in the stopping action so that the outside leg is ready and in position for the quick thrust in the new direction.

The Quick Break

Hockey is a game of quick breaks. Slow skaters can gain an advantage over the opposition with quick breaks. Quick breaks get the jump on the opposition by beating an opponent and getting to the puck first. Good players are able to break quickly from a dead stop, a coasting position and a full stride.

For the quick break, lean well forward and get good flexion or bend to the knees so that the legs can achieve an explosive thrusting action. Each leg, in turn, moves as fast as possible. Often the start is with short strides, and as speed picks up, the stride will lengthen. Some players do a series of hops or runs to get started. This looks stylish but is not as effective as good natural skating action.

Scooting

Scooting or scootering is just what the name implies – moving as if one was on a scooter. The skill is simply gliding on one leg and using the other leg for a series of pushes. This skill is very useful in close quarters, especially along the boards. Scooting will give you a solid base and yet provide power and progression. Many players will cut around a defenseman by sticking one leg in front, the other leg back to protect the puck and then coast around the defenseman. By scooting around the defenseman, an attacker will be able to maintain speed, have more power and still be able to protect the puck. Scooting is not a common skill but it can be valuable as it is another trick or deception in your bag of tricks.

Change of Pace

The change of pace is another good skill to master as the opposition will have difficulty in reading your speed and maneuvers. There are many ways to change pace. Perhaps the most deceptive changes are the quick break and the quick-slow-quick routine. In the quick break, the trick is in the first push – it must be quick and powerful. The slow part of the quick-slow-quick routine can be performed by eliminating or almost eliminating the pushing or thrusting phase of the skating action. Eliminating the thrust can be achieved by not digging the skate blades into the ice. The change of pace is of no value unless it is executed precisely, not only in execution but also in timing. Try the change of pace too soon or too late, and you are in trouble. Practice under different conditions will develop the timing skill.

II. Puck Control

Puck Control involves stickhandling, passing, pass receiving and shooting. Puck control is second in importance only to the skill of skating. The skills of puck control are vital to organizing and controlling the game. Team strategy is dependent on puck control. Poor passing and pass receiving will weaken the attack and nullify scoring opportunities. The team that can control the puck will control the game.

The Hockey Stick

The correct lie for the hockey stick will depend on the height, body lean and skating style of the player. Trying various lies of the hockey sticks when practicing is perhaps the best method for determining which lie is best for you. Experiment – you may be surprised which lie works best. Very often you can tell from the wearing of the stick blade. If the heel of the blade is overly worn then the lie may be too upright. If the toe is more worn than usual then the stick may be too low a lie.

Experiment with the length of your hockey stick. An old criterion used to be that the length of the stick should be from the floor to the chin of the player. This may be a basis to start from, but stick length should be determined by the height, body lean and skating stride of the player. Try not to get used to cutting too much from the hockey stick. A shorter stick may give you more control, but it also takes away leverage from the stick. The leverage helps to give power to your shot. Usually the more upright the lie, the shorter the hockey stick; as the more upright lie brings the puck into play closer to the player's body. Experiment with both styles and get the feel for each.

Stickhandling

Stickhandling is fading in importance in current hockey play because the emphasis is on a strong passing game and the strategy of shooting the puck into the corner and chasing it. Despite this strategy, good stickhandlers will always be in demand. The better players in any league are usually the better stickhandlers. Many youngsters are discouraged from stickhandling by coaches who put so much emphasis on winning that they forget to develop the skills of the players. Youngsters, especially those who are not skilled in stickhandling, are very often discouraged in using this skill during a game on the grounds that they will lose the puck to the opposition. Some coaches would rather have the poorer skilled players get the puck to the better players or shoot the puck into the end zone. This strategy may have merit, but it does not help in developing young players' puck control.

Stickhandling is a delicate art. It requires coordination with an uncanny "feel" for the puck while not even watching the puck. You also must be able to control the puck to each side of the body and not just in front of the body. The puck must also be moved from one side to the other side in one continuous sweep. When sweeping the puck from side to side the toe the blade must be "toed in" so that the puck does not slip off the end of the stick blade.

When stickhandling the player should hold his arms out in front of his body so that he will have good freedom of arm movement. Many players keep their arms too close to their body, and as a result, they restrict their arm movement and their control of the puck. The puck is moved in a smooth and easy manner, 'feathered' from point to point, not slammed. The stick is to be lightly placed on the ice with the puck, not smashed to the ice in an uncontrolled manner. Stickhandling is simply passing and pass receiving with yourself. You must practice this skill on each side of the body as well as in front of the body.

The puck is controlled by feel and not by sight. Occasional peeks at the puck may be harmless, but one should not rely on "puck peeking." Your eyesight is needed for looking around and analyzing the situation. Some players are able to control the puck but lack confidence in looking up while doing it, so practice with the head up is essential. As the skill improves, so will confidence. Be prepared to put in the time during practice. It will get better.

Good coaching is very important to developing good stickhandling, not so much in the teaching of the skill but in the encouragement of the player. The coach must let the players try the skill under game conditions so that development will occur. The coach must show confidence in his players and encourage them to have faith in their abilities.

Another skill youngsters should practice while stickhandling is the ability to shoot and pass without changing the skating stride or giving the puck an adjustment before the shot or pass. Many players telegraph their shot or pass by adjusting their feet so they can shoot or pass off their strong leg. Others will give the puck a little adjustment to prepare for the shot or pass. To be a good stickhandler with deceptive tactics, young hockey players must learn to shoot and pass in stride with no adjusting of the feet and no adjustment of the puck. Learning this skill when young will show great dividends as the player advances in age and playing levels.

Passing

THE DIRECTION OF THE PASS

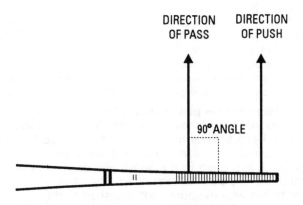

Diagram 2-1

The direction of the pass (diagram 2-1) is determined by two factors: the direction of the push on the stick and the angle of the stick blade. To pass to the target, the player must simply push the stick blade in the direction of the target. This sounds simple. Unfortunately, the failure to push the stick straight to the target is the reason for most inaccurate passes. Look at diagram 2-2.

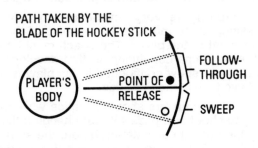

INCORRECT

Diagram 2-2

Notice the path of the arms and the hockey stick and how they swing around the body in an arc of a circle. If the arms swing in a circular pattern, the hockey stick blade will also swing in a circular pattern. To achieve accuracy from this circular pattern, the puck must be released at exactly the right angle to the target. If the puck is not released at this precise point, then the pass will be inaccurate. There are usually two reasons why the player lets the stick prescribe this circular pattern. One is that the player is careless in execution, and the second is that the player lets the arms remain at the same length throughout the pass. In diagram 2-3, notice the difference in the path of the hockey stick blade.

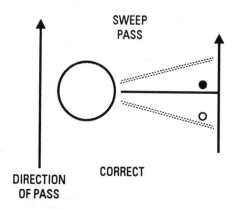

SWEEP
PASS

CORRECT

DIRECTION
OF PASS

Diagram 2-3

In the correct passing action, the sweep and follow through of the stick blade move straight to the target. When the stick blade is moved at right angles to the target the puck can be released at various points of the sweep and still be in line with the target. To achieve this straight line passing action to the target, the arms move from fairly close to the body to an extended position away from the body. The arms push the whole stick to the target. Watch a professional hockey player pass, and you will notice how both arms are involved in the pass. Both arms push the hockey stick. Watch a poor passer, and often you will see how the top arm of the hockey stick is jammed into the body and the lower arm swings the stick around the body for the pass.

The key to the square pass is in the movement of the top hand on the hockey stick. The passer must move the top hand along with the bottom hand in the direction of the pass. The top hand will move about the same distance toward the target as the lower hand. If the passer lets the top hand remain jammed to his body then the hockey stick blade will take on the characteristics of a circular passing movement as in diagram 2-2.

When passing, body balance is very important. The body must not fall away or backward from the pass. Such action may well destroy accuracy as the falling action destroys the hockey stick blade's straight line to the target. The head should not move or shift while passing. A stationary head helps to maintain body control.

Types of Passes

THE SWEEP PASS

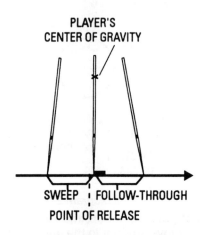

Diagram 2-4

Diagram 2-4 shows the action of the hockey stick in executing the sweep pass, the basic pass in hockey. Notice the 'X' in the diagram. The 'X' is the shooter's center of gravity or his balance point. This is also the point of the hockey stick being in a perpendicular position. It is this position that is best for releasing the puck. If the release is too late into the follow-through, the blade will be slanted back and cause the puck to lift, flip or roll. Keep the follow-through low and to the target.

Diagram 2-5 is looking at diagram 2-4 from the top view. Passing and shooting have the same mechanics. The puck is released at the player's center of gravity. This center of gravity release is on an imaginary line drawn from the point of release, square or perpendicular to the direction of the pass. If this criteria is accomplished then the pass or shot should be well executed. If the body falls away from the shot, then the center of gravity or balance point on the shot or pass is changed, and the result is inefficient.

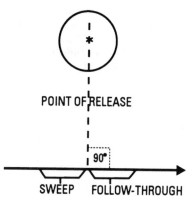

Diagram 2-5

THE SLAP PASS

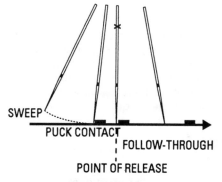

Diagram 2-6

All types of passes basically employ the mechanics similar to the sweep pass. The slap pass (diagram 2-6) is much like the sweep pass except the puck is not in contact with the blade of the stick during the sweep. The blade makes contact with the puck just prior to the point of release. On the sweep pass, the blade rides along the ice with the puck to the point of release. In the slap pass, the blade is off the ice and swings down to the puck much like a golf shot.

THE QUICK WRIST PASS

The quick wrist pass is a very short sweep pass with emphasis on the action of the wrists. The mechanics are similar to the sweep pass except that the sweep and follow-through are much shorter. With the shorter sweep, it is more difficult to build up power, but it can be done with strong wrist and arm action.

THE LIFT PASS

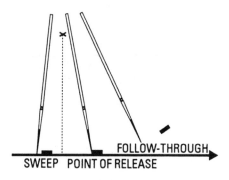

Diagram 2-7

The lift pass in diagram 2-7 is used to pass over an obstacle or obstruction. This is accomplished by releasing the puck well past the center of gravity point. The hockey stick will also be falling backward from a vertical to a more horizontal position. The follow-through will be higher. To get a higher lift pass, it may help to snap the top hand back to get a quicker and higher elevation to the puck.

THE FLIP PASS

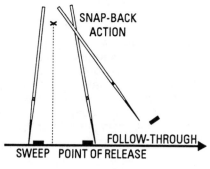

Diagram 2-8

This is another type of lift pass. The stick blade is laid flatter, the arms give a push, the wrist give a snap and the puck is flipped up in the air. This pass has a very vertical flight path, and on landing, the puck will have less sliding action. This pass can be used to move the puck out of a congested area so that quick wingers can pick it up before an icing call.

THE BACKHAND PASS

Hockey players should be able to pass the puck efficiently in a forehand or backhand manner to any direction. The mechanics of the backhand are similar to the forehand except the hands are pulled rather than pushed.

THE DROP PASS AND BACK PASS

The drop pass and back pass are similar except the back pass passes the puck backward while the drop pass leaves the puck in a stationary position with no movement.

For the drop pass, the player brings the puck to the side of his body. The puck is moving forward at the same speed as the player. The player then places the blade of the stick in front of the puck to prevent forward movement of the puck. As the body is moving forward, the stick blade remains stationary so that the puck does not move. The puck is held on the same spot on the ice by the stick blade as the body skates past the puck.

The back pass is executed in the same manner except the blade of the stick is pulled back to give the puck backward movement. The speed of the back pass will depend on how hard the hands are pulled back. It is important to keep the blade perpendicular to the direction of the pass and to not let the blade of the stick flip or roll the puck.

Aiming the Pass

To pass accurately, the pass must lead the receiver. The amount of lead will depend on the speed of the receiver or target and the distance or length of the pass. The pass should be aimed at the stick blade of the receiver and not aimed at the player's body. For this reason, pass receivers should have their stick on the ice to provide a target to aim at.

BLIND PASS

There should be no pass unless there is a team-mate there or there will be one there to receive the pass. Blind passes are dangerous and often turn into an advantage for the other team. Therefore, do not pass and hope a team-mate is there. Be certain on all passes.

WHEN TO PASS

Passes are made to gain an advantage. For every pass your team makes, the opposition has to make an adjustment. The more passes a team makes, the more adjustments the opposition has to make. If the opposition is forced into enough adjustments then eventually they will make a mistake or break down. When the opposition makes a mistake, the attacking team has a chance to take advantage of the opposition's weaknesses.

Pass Receiving

When receiving a pass, the blade of the pass receiver's hockey stick should be square to the direction of the pass. The stick blade should also provide a little cushion or "give" during contact with the puck. It also helps to cup the stick blade over the puck at contact to help prevent any chance of the puck jumping over the stick blade.

When pass receiving, do not take your eyes off the puck until you have it under control. Some players look up just a little too soon. Another problem many youth players have in pass receiving is that they deflect the puck ahead of them and then skate after it. Do not do this. Players do this because they lack skill in receiving a pass. Learn to control the puck when it is passed to you.

The pass receiver should give the passer a target to aim at by putting the blade of his stick where the pass is wanted. The stick blade is a good target, especially for quick shots on goal or deflected passes to another team-mate. With the blade on the ice, the pass receiver also indicates that he is ready to receive the pass. It is the duty of the pass receiver to put himself in position to receive the pass. Good pass receivers can take a pass on the forehand, backhand and from any angle.

Some passes are not perfect and the receiver may have to adjust for the imperfect pass. Several techniques can be used. If the pass is in the feet, the skate blade can deflect the puck up to your stick. On some passes, slowing down or speeding up may be required. Often if the pass is at the feet, slowing down can give the puck time to get in front. Speeding up may help you get in position for the pass that is made too far ahead of you. Sometimes drifting and cutting will have the same effect for the poor passes. Youth players must practice receiving imperfect passes because, under game conditions, most passes will not be perfect.

Shooting

Shooting is the final phase of goal scoring. Passing and skating put the puck into a scoring situation, but it is the shot on goal that determines whether it is a goal or just another attempt. Scoring opportunities are scarce. When the opportunity presents itself, one must capitalize on the situation. Many games have been won by teams that were able to make the most of their scoring opportunities despite being outplayed and outshot.

Shooting mechanics are similar to passing. The shooters hands are spread a little more on the hockey stick than when stickhandling. This gives more power to your shot. The body leans forward and the weight of the body is on the front leg (the left leg for the right hand shot). During the shooting action, the shooter must maintain body lean forward and must not let his body fall back. Falling back will weaken the shot and give poor accuracy. Also, do not let the shoulder of the top hand on the hockey stick (the front shoulder) pull away from the shot. This is a common mistake. The pulling away of the shoulder is like the falling back on the shot as both give loss of power and accuracy.

Types of Shots

THE SWEEP OR WRIST SHOT

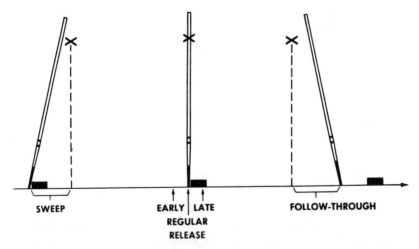

Figure 2-9

This is the basic shot in hockey. It is powerful and accurate, as well as easy to control. This shot can be performed quickly which is a shooter's advantage in giving the goaltender less time to read the shot. The length of the sweep, the downward force exerted on the stick and the speed of the forward movement of the hands are factors determining the speed of the shot.

The puck is played much like the sweep pass. The body is leaned forward; the front leg (left leg for right shot) carries the body weight, and the blade of the stick is cupped over the puck. The sweep begins with the arms sweeping forward and downward towards the target. As the puck is swept forward, the puck is released at the center of gravity by a strong wrist snap. The blade of the stick continues into the follow-through. The release point will determine the height of the shot. Early release is a low shot, and a late release is high shot. Throughout the shot, the body remains forward. The front shoulder and body do not fall away from the shot at any time. A common problem for poor shooters and beginners is that they position the puck too far in front of their body. This is done with the incorrect intent of making it easier to lift the puck. This positioning of the puck fails to put power into the shot. Good shooters sweep the puck from a line behind their body to the front of their body. Many times under game conditions the player does not have space for a long sweep. No problem, just use a short sweep and follow-through with the same mechanics.

THE SLAP SHOT

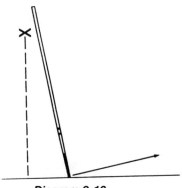

Diagram 2-10

The slap shot is similar to the sweep shot. In the sweep shot, the puck is in contact with the stick blade for the entire sweep along the ice. In the slap shot, the sweep is off the ice and meets the puck prior to its release position. On meeting the puck, the stick is forced into the ice and through the point of release.

Good shooters practice for accuracy and power. If you want to be a good slap shot shooter then you must practice for accuracy with power. Shoot to a variety of targets. Shorten your backswing if it is a little long. Stay over the shot and do not pull away with the front shoulder or let your body fall away from the shot. Keep your head down and watch the puck being hit with the stick.

Do not be worried about loss of power by shortening the backswing for the slap shot. Many players find that they can accelerate faster through the puck by using a shorter backswing. Many find that they have better balance with the shorter backswing. The shorter backswing means the puck is shot on goal much quicker and usually more accurately. The quicker shot means the goaltender must react sooner and has less time to read or prepare for the shot.

THE WRIST SLAP SHOT

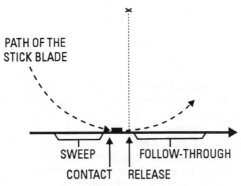

PATH OF THE
STICK BLADE

SWEEP   CONTACT   RELEASE   FOLLOW-THROUGH

Diagram 2-11

The wrist slap shot is a valuable shot to have in your skill bag. It is a combination of the wrist or sweep shot and the slap shot. The sweep for the wrist slap shot is very short and is performed without the puck. The puck is contacted just prior to release as described in the slap shot. At puck contact, the stick blade is driven into the ice and the wrists give a strong snap-action to propel the puck forward. The follow-through is short.

THE FLIP SHOT

The flip shot is the same as the flip pass. It can be very useful when the goalie is down and you want to flip the puck over his sprawling body. The flip shot enable you to get the puck up into a high trajectory as quickly as possible. Power is not important to this shot, finesse is crucial. The flip shot is often used to land in front of the goaltender so that it hits the ice and takes a crazy bounce. Sometimes these crazy bounces go into the goal and sometimes they do not, but they do drive the goaltender crazy and make him nervous.

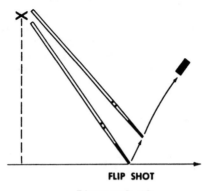

FLIP SHOT

Diagram 2 -12

THE BACKHAND SHOT

The value of the backhand shot is that the goaltender often has a difficult time reading the shot. Also, there are many times during a game when the shooter's body cannot be positioned for the forehand shot. On backhand shots, the shooter's mechanics change, and the puck comes off the stick differently than with the forehand shot. The mechanics of the backhand are the same as the forehand except the puck is shot by a pulling action of the arms. The pulling action of the arms is what gives the goaltender difficulty in reading the backhand shot.

SHOT VARIATIONS

Under game conditions, you may not be able to execute the various shots exactly as described. You may also have variations to the mechanics. Sometimes you will be off-balance or you may be in congestion, but, whatever the problem, you must get the shot away. You must shoot off either foot and with no adjustments of your feet. The better your basic mechanics, the better your shot on goal despite interference.

In shooting, experiment to find the best part of the stick blade to shoot the puck. Some players like the puck on the toe, some like the middle and others like the heel. Some players vary the puck placement on the blade for different types of shots. Many find the heel is best for the slap and the toe for the wrist slap shot. Some even find the opposite works best for them. Experiment to find which is best for you. Young hockey players must realize that they will not always be able to get desired puck placement, so they must learn to shoot the puck from all positions on the blade of the stick.

Achieving Power in Shooting and Passing

Power in the shot and pass is governed by three factors: (1) downward force, (2) length of sweep, and (3) speed of hands and arms.

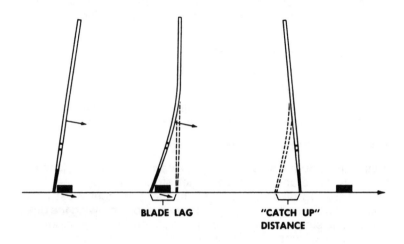

BLADE LAG   "CATCH UP"
DISTANCE

Diagram 2-13

DOWNWARD FORCE

When shooting the puck, the hockey stick is forced into the ice, and the shaft of the stick is bent. You must bend the shaft of the stick to get power in the shot. The bending of the shaft causes blade lag. Blade lag is when the blade of the stick lags behind the upper shaft of the stick. As the stick moves forward, the blade springs forward to 'catch up' with the upper part of the shaft. This 'catch up' action increases the speed of the stick blade and increases the speed of the shot. 'Catch up' speed is determined by the amount of downward force, the bend of the stick and the stiffness of the shaft. The more bend, the more 'catch up' distance. The stiffer the shaft, the faster the stick will spring back to a straight shaft.

As a hockey player you should select a stick that will give you the best combination of these factors. Too whippy a stick will produce plenty of bend but will also give you slow 'catch up' speed. Too stiff a stick will be difficult to bend and thus give you little 'catch up' distance. You need a stick to satisfy your strength and style. Your stick must be stiff enough to provide good 'catch up' speed but whippy enough to give good bend.

LENGTH OF SWEEP

The longer the sweep, the greater the speed and momentum that can be built up prior to release of the puck. However, too long a backswing is actually cumbersome and often not an increase in power. Under game conditions the shorter backswing is advantageous in getting the shot away quicker.

SPEED OF HANDS AND ARMS

The faster the hands and arms move into the shot, the greater the resulting speed of the puck.

Good powerful shooters execute all three of these factors. Downward force is critical to power in the shot. Practice it.

Beating a Checker while Controlling the Puck

Many times during a game, the puck carrier will be unable to pass to a team-mate and will have to get around an opponent by his own means. To do this successfully, the opponent must be deceived. This deception is known as "deking" or "throwing the deke." The deke is simply a trick, fake or deception to fool an opponent. Good dekes require good puck control and skating agility.

The timing of the deke is vital to execution. If the deke is too close to the opponent, the attacker will not have enough time to complete the deke and may even run into his opponent. If the deke is too far away from the opponent, the opponent has time to react to the deke. Timing will depend on the moving speed of the attacker and opponent and the type of deke. If anything, the deke should be executed a little early rather than late. A late deke almost has no chance. An early deke may still have a chance. Experience and practice is essential in learning how to time the deke. Do not be discouraged by unsuccessful attempts as this is just part of the learning process. Keep practicing.

In throwing the deke, look for signs that you have fooled or deceived your opponent. If your opponent is not deceived then another deke may be needed. Things move fast, so sometimes a good deke may not work. Just keep at it. Eventually you will fool the opposition. The following are some sample dekes and deceptions. When deking, it is imperative not to over-emphasize the deceptive trick. For example, some players, when doing the shoulder drop, make it too excessive and the opposition knows it is a trick. Subtle deception is best. Practice many of the following tricks and learn to use them under game conditions. Learn to be a deceptive hockey player.

THE SHOULDER DROP

A puck carrier, when closing in on his opponent, can drop a shoulder and give the upper body a little twist in the direction of the shoulder drop. The opponent may think the attacker is going in that direction and move to counter the attacker. When the defender makes his move to cover the attacker, the attacker simply changes his direction. The shoulder drop is one of the most simple tricks, yet it is very effective.

THE CROSS-OVER

As the attacker approaches the defender, he crosses one leg over the other as if turning in that direction. When the defender makes his counter move, the attacker changes directions. It is important that when the attacker makes his move to the new direction, the first several skating thrusts must be strong and fast to get around the defender quickly. The defender must not be given a chance to recover.

THE BODY WEAVE

The body weave is simply weaving or twisting the body to each side to confuse an opponent. The side of the opponent to which the attacker will go will depend on the moves of the opponent. Sometimes an opponent is caught flat-footed and the attacker can go to either side.

THE ZIG-ZAG

The zig-zag can be performed by using the cross-overs, body weaves or a combination of both. The idea is to approach the defender in a zig-zag manner so that he is confused as to whether you will zig next or zag next.

THE SIDE JUMP

The side jump is used to quickly move out of the way of an opponent or body check. It's effectiveness is in the quickness of execution as the side jump is delayed until very close to the defender.

THE DRAW-A-WAY

This is performed in much the same way as the side jump; except that the player, instead of jumping to the side, will slip past his opponent by turning sideways. In some situations the extra distance from the defender may not need the sideways jump.

THE CHANGE OF PACE

The change of pace is simply using various speeds to deceive the defender. The change of pace is also very effective with the other deceptive tricks in this chapter.

THE FAST BREAK

The fast break is a change of pace tactic. If the attacker has the speed or the defender is flat-footed, then the fast break may be all one needs to beat a defender.

THE STOP AND GO

The stop and go is also a change of pace. The weak part of this deception is the stop. If the attacker is not careful, the stop will give the defender time to check the attacker. The go part also has to be very quick. This trick will usually not work with the defender facing you. It is best when the opponent is chasing you from the side or from behind. When done properly, the opponent will skate by you. This may not always be good since the opponent chasing you will then be in the way of your forward progression and you will have to beat him again.

THE FAKE SHOT AND FAKE PASS

The fake shot and fake pass can be very effective if timed properly. The fake shot or fake pass may just get the defender to make a move to cover the intended pass. A slight hesitation by the defender may be just enough time for an attacker to beat the defender.

VARIETY OF TRICKS

Good deceptive hockey players do not become predictable in their tricks. With this in mind, young hockey players must realize the importance of having a variety of tricks to beat an opponent. The tricks or dekes listed in this chapter are only some of the tricks used by hockey players. There are many variations of the ones listed. Learn them and practice them. They are valuable.

PROTECTING THE PUCK AFTER THE DEKE

The key is to keep the puck as far as possible from the defender. Some players spread the legs for stability as it makes it harder for the defender to reach around for the puck. Notice how the puck carrier has his body always between the puck and the defender. To get the puck, the defender is in a difficult position as he must go through the puck carrier or around the puck carrier.

III. Goaltending

Goaltenders must exemplify the following characteristics:

1. Agility and coordination
2. Skating ability
3. Reflexes and eyesight
4. Hockey sense and hockey intelligence
5. Anticipation
6. Physical and mental courage

The Stance

A goaltender must move with explosive action in all directions. To achieve maximum efficiency for these moves, the goaltender must have a solid, strong and well-balanced base. Diagram 3-1 shows how the body is balanced. A good stance provides the necessary foundation. A poor stance gives a weak base and puts the body in a poor position for quick moves. The delay may only be a split second, but for a goaltender, the split second delay can be devastating.

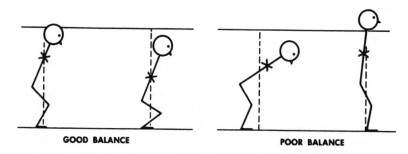

GOOD BALANCE   POOR BALANCE

Diagram 3-1

The proper stance consists of spreading the feet and squatting. Body weight is balanced over the skate blades. The spread of the feet will depend on the feel and style of the goaltender. Trial and error practice will help determine the position from which the goalie can make the quickest moves in any direction. Whether the squat is low or high, the center of gravity or balance point must be over the center of your skate blades and between the two skates. If the balance point is in front or behind the skate blades, the goaltender will be in poor balance for moves in any direction.

When in the squat position, it is important to have good flex to the ankles, knees and hips. The deeper the squat, the more the bend to all three joints. Lack of flexibility in any of the joints will contribute to a weak stance.

In the squat position, good goaltenders will slightly knock their knees in toward each other to provide a strong position for lateral movement to either side. If the knees are bowed out or straight, the knee must be knocked inward for the thrust to the side. This results in a slower reaction time.

The following guidelines will help determine a goaltender's stance. The arms should hang comfortably to the side of the legs. The shoulders should be loose, natural and strong. The shoulders must not hunch or droop. The spine is fairly straight, as is the neck, so that the head is up and not drooping down. The correct stance will give a good breathing position and will not restrict the inhale and exhale action of the lungs. Body weight should be evenly distributed to both feet. The head must be up for good visibility.

The stick blade should be held flat on the ice and a little in front of the toes. By keeping the blade of the stick away from toes, the goaltender is able to cushion a shot that strikes the goal stick. The catching glove should be open, facing the puck, low and ready to move up quickly. The knees are slightly knocked in toward each other to put the skate blades in an angled position for thrusting to the side.

Lateral Movement

Good goaltenders move laterally (to the side) quickly and efficiently. They are also in balance after the move in case they have to make another move in another direction. The lateral move may well be one of the keys to a goaltender's success.

In moving to the side (laterally), the leg farthest from the direction of travel will initiate the move. Diagram 3-2 shows how the goaltender moves to the side. The action of the thrusting leg is to bend (adduct) inward at the knee and force the skate blade into the ice for a hard push. The greater the force applied, the more explosive the move to the side. Unless the knee is bent, the leg is unable to dig the skate blade into the ice for a strong and powerful thrust. By standing with the knees slightly knocked inward, the goaltender is in the ready position for sideward movement in either direction. There is no time delay of adducting the knees before moving.

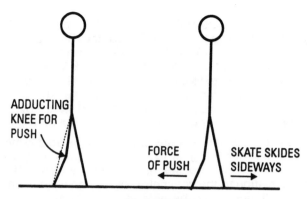

Diagram 3-2

In this ready stance, both legs should be resisting each other from thrusting to the side. If the resistance of one leg is taken away the goaltender will automatically move to the side. Coaches and/ or the goaltenders themselves should check the stance to see if the body moves to the side when one leg is lifted.

The Glide Across

The glide across is the stand-up gliding action of the goaltender as he moves to the side to jockey for position and cut the angle of the shot on goal. The glide across is much like backward skating with the heel leading the direction of travel. The movement is initiated by the hips and upper thighs swinging toward the direction of travel. While the hips are moving, the far leg is thrusting to push the body in the desired direction. The near skate rotates in the direction of travel so that the heel leads the gliding action. The near leg also provides the balance and stability as the far leg is thrusting. While the body is gliding to the side, the shoulders, glove and stick remain square to the puck and ready for action. The head is up and facing the puck.

EDGE VIEW (ENLARGED) OF PRACTICE SHOOTING BOARD

Diagram 3-3

Diagram 3-3 shows the action of the skate blade. At the start, the left leg is thrusting and the right leg is gliding. Both legs then glide until the right leg skate makes the move to stop. To stop the glide, the goaltender should swing the stopping leg's knee outward with the lower leg and skate following the knee until the skate blade is perpendicular to the direction of travel. As the skate blade moves into the perpendicular position, a downward force by the stopping leg will help the skate blade dig into the ice for a quick stop.

With this gliding action, a goaltender should be able to move from any spot in front of the goal to either goal post in one efficient thrust and glide. Good goalies have an awareness of their body position in relation to the goal net. This awareness must be developed. A goaltender must be able to move from any position in front of the goal net to either goal post without looking for the goal post. The eyes must be on the puck, not the direction in which the body is moving. Goaltenders must practice orientation with the goal net. Excellent practice can be accomplished even while no one is shooting. This can be practiced by moving around the goal area and back to the goal post while looking straight ahead. The face-off circles, the corners, the markings on the boards all help in giving an awareness of where the goal net and goal posts are located.

The Side Kick

The side kick is throwing the leg out at the puck while the body remains upright. As the leg is thrown at the puck, the opposite leg thrusts into the ice to assist and speed up the thrown leg. Sometimes the thrusting leg will drop to the ice but the body should still remain upright if possible. The side kick action is not always desirable to stop a puck along the ice as it is very difficult to keep the leg flat on the ice to catch the puck. If possible, it is usually best to use the stick to stop the puck along the ice. It is important to maintain balance while throwing the leg out at the puck so that the body is still ready to react in a new direction. Some goaltenders throw the leg out and then fall to the ice, off-balance and out of position for any type of recovery. This must be eliminated. The side kick is a valuable skill, but you must use it at the right time. For shots along the ice, use your stick. For shots off the ice, use the leg, but remain in balance for the next move.

The Sprawling Slide

The sprawling slide is a very dangerous move for a goaltender. It is a diving action with the feet leading or the head leading. The sprawling slide is a desperation move and so the goaltender must use it as a last resort. It is acceptable if the puck is stopped and controlled by the goaltender. The big danger in the sprawling slide is that the goaltender is out of position, off-balance and not ready for a rebound shot. It is very easy for the goaltender to become a "sitting duck" after a sprawling slide. Very often goaltenders, when sliding out feet first, bounce their legs off the ice. With the legs bouncing off the ice, the puck can very easily slide under the goaltender's legs and into the net. Once the goaltender makes the sprawling slide, he is committed to the action; there is no recovery. If this slide becomes common to a goalie, the attackers will quickly take advantage of this by faking or tricking the goaltender into making a sprawling move. Remember, goalies must make the move to the puck, but the goalie should make the move that leaves him in position for the next move. Goaltenders must not let themselves develop the habit of being a sprawler.

The One-Knee Slide

The one-knee slide is performed by the thrusting leg's knee dropping to the ice after the thrust. The gliding leg remains upright. The sliding leg must be flat on the ice and the knee should be touching the heel of the gliding leg's foot to prevent an opening between the legs. The body action is similar to a baseball player going down on one knee to block an unpredictable ground ball. An advantage of the one-knee slide is that the goaltender provides a large blocking area to the shooter. Also, the goaltender is in position to change directions quickly and efficiently. To change directions the goaltender simply lifts the knee of the sliding leg and thrusts with the gliding leg to the new direction.

The Goalkeeper's Body and Equipment

THE GLOVE HAND

The glove hand is the hand wearing the catching glove. The skill of catching the puck is similar to catching a ball with a baseball glove. Goaltenders must watch the puck until it is caught. Taking the eyes off the puck or losing focus of the puck will result in carelessness in catching the puck. In most cases, you will find it best to hold the glove hand low and facing the puck. It is easier and quicker to move your glove up than it is to move your glove lower or downward to catch the puck.

The advantage of the glove hand over the blocking glove is that the glove controls the puck by catching it so there is no rebounds or deflections. When a goaltender catches the puck, the glove and puck should be brought into the front of the body, usually the chest area, for protection. When moving the glove hand after the catch, it is advisable to swing your hand with a stiff wrist action. If your wrist is allowed to flip or flick, it is possible for the puck to slip out, or be thrown out, of the glove and perhaps into the net.

THE BLOCKING HAND

The blocking hand holds the goal stick and is protected by a large flat pad. The blocker, if properly used, can be valuable in deflecting shots into the corners. In most cases, the shots have to be defected because the flat surface makes it difficult to bring the puck under control. The large surface of the blocker can make it advantageous for deflecting the puck. The weight of the goal stick and blocker can hamper speed of movement. Moving the stick and blocker should be performed by the large muscles of the upper arms and shoulders. Coaches should develop specific practice drills to improve the blocking action of goaltenders. Goaltenders must realize the importance of physical strength in moving around the goal and stopping shots. If you want to be a goaltender, a weight training program can be helpful. Strong goaltenders move quicker and better.

THE GOAL STICK

The goal stick is usually the best means of stopping shots along the ice. Sometimes the skate blade or the goal pad down on the ice is effective if the stick is out of position; however, the skate blade or goal pad does not have control of the puck like the goal stick. The goal stick can deflect the puck at any desired angle or can cushion the puck with a little give to the stick. Cushioning the puck with the stick can leave the puck under control for the goaltender. Controlling the puck with the stick also leaves the puck in position for a pass to a teammate or a clearing shot by the goaltender. In fact, a break-out play can be effectively organized by starting with a pass from the goaltender.

In stopping shots along the ice, the goaltender must learn to slide the goal stick in either direction with the blade remaining flat on the ice. In sliding the stick to the side, it is best to keep the stick perpendicular to the ice. If the stick is allowed to lean back while moving to the side, the puck can deflect up and over the stick blade and into the goal net. It is a natural reaction for the goal stick to lean away from the shot as the stick is moved to the side. The proper movement of the goal stick is a difficult skill but it must be mastered.

THE LEGS

The goal pads are mainly used for blocking purposes. The goaltender must make the goal pads part of him so that the pads do not impede movement and agility. Goaltenders must be physically strong to manipulate the large pads. Good goaltenders are able to deflect the puck to a desired direction. This skill must be learned to prevent rebounds from bouncing back to the opposition. Good deflection can deflect the puck to a team-mate. It is also desirable for the goaltender to be able to cushion the puck on contact with the goal pads. This skill will drop the puck to the goaltenders feet so that he can pass the puck with the stick or push the puck with the skate blade to a controlled position.

THE BODY

The body is used for blocking purposes, to smother shots and protect the puck when necessary. The body should be moved behind the shot whenever possible as a means of backup protection. The body is often the main line of defense as it used to cut down the angle of shots. The body moves forward to block out the net on the shooter. The hands, stick, and blocker look spectacular when making the save but it is the body that positions itself to give the shooter no angle and difficulty in scoring goals. Goal net orientation and playing the angle is about the body being in position for the shots on goal.

Goal Net Orientation

In order to be in position to play the angle, the goaltender must have an excellent orientation of exactly where the goal net is while looking at the puck and not towards the goal. Goaltenders must be able to move around, from side to side, forward and backwards and still be able to place their body in a position to bisect a line from the puck to the center of the goal net. A goaltender must be able to move out to cut the angle and then move back to the goalpost without looking back. Goal net orientation is a difficult skill and takes time to learn. Coaches must provide drills to help goaltenders develop this demanding skill.

To help orientation, goaltenders often use their hands and goal stick to feel for the goal post. The glove hand can be swung back quickly to feel or hit the post. The top of the goal stick shaft can be swung back to strike the goal post. The stick blade can also be used in a similar manner. Markings on the rink boards, like the angle to the blue line on the boards help in orientation by giving a feel for one's position on the ice. Very often goaltenders have difficulty when playing away from their home rink. The unfamiliarity of the rink and surroundings may give the goaltender difficulty with his orientation. When playing an unfamiliar rink take time before the game to get the feel of the rink markings. Look at the possible angles for shots. Draw imaginary lines if necessary. Practice your moves around the net to get the feel of location. Do not leave anything to chance.

Positional Play or Playing the Angle

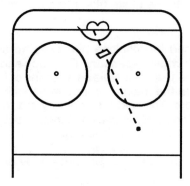

Diagram 3-4

The goaltender must position himself in relation to the puck and
the goal net. This means that the body bisects a line from the puck
to the center of the goal net (diagram 3-4). On this line, the
goaltender moves out or away from the net or back towards the
net. It is this movement away from the goal net and back to the
goal net that positions the goaltender for cutting the angle.

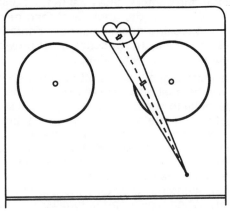

Diagram 3-5

When moving out, the goalie's body is able to block more of the
net to give the shooter less net to shoot at. Diagram 3-4 shows
how the line from the puck to the center of the goal net is bisected
by the goaltender's body. Diagram 3-5 shows a dashed line from

the puck to the center of the goal net and how the goaltender moves out to cut the angle. The two solid lines determine the boundary lines from the puck to the goal. The puck must remain inside these lines to hit the goal. Notice how the openings to the goal get smaller as the goaltender moves out toward the puck.

It is readily noticeable how a goaltender gives the shooter less net to shoot at by moving toward the puck. In game conditions, the goaltender must decide how far he can move out without leaving himself vulnerable behind. Naturally, the situation will determine how far from the net the goalie may move. If the goalie moves too far out, he leaves the net exposed to the non-puck carrying players to receive a pass or tip-in. Very often a goaltender will hang close to the net and then take a quick move out when he is certain the puck will be shot on goal.

Goaltenders must focus not only on the puck, but they must also be aware of the total play and the positioning of all attackers. This awareness will help develop anticipation of the play. This anticipation sense is difficult to develop, but it must be practiced. Good goaltenders have learned anticipation through experience. Good goaltenders know that their positional play is the criteria for success. Being in position makes the play of the goal stick, the glove hand and the blocker just that much easier. Speed of the hands and legs do not make up for poor positional play. To be a goaltender, you must continually work with your positional play and orientation with the goal net and puck.

General Rules

As a goaltender, you must focus on the puck but keep pace with the whole attack and the position of all attackers. Learn to read the play as it develops. This will help you make better decisions on how to counter the attack. When it looks like a shot is coming on net, study the shooter and the shooter's stick. Experience will help you read the coming shot. The movement of the shooter's body and stick often give clues as to a shot's direction. Some signs of possible shots coming to the net are indicated by the shoulder and arm movement, the lifting of a leg, the head dropping for a slap shot, and a change in the skating stride. You must not only be alert to these clues but you must be prepared for the fake shot, deke or other deceptive moves.

Try to remain in a stand-up position as much as possible. The stand-up position will give you the best blocking area of the goal net and keep you in position to move to any new position. When it is necessary to go down, the one-knee drop is usually the most advantageous move. The one-knee drop gives good blocking area and also puts you in good position to change directions or move to a new position. Some goaltenders like the two-knee drop, and it can be effective. However, it may be difficult to get up quickly or make a recovery move. In most cases, it is best to keep the knees together with the skates apart to give the legs a little more blocking area. The two-knee drop should not be used until the skill of standing up quickly after the two-knee drop is mastered. Good goalies that use the two-knee drop rock back slightly with the upper body to balance over their skates and then lift up their body by bringing both legs together. This powerful move requires practice. You can practice this skill without wearing your goal equipment.

The sharpness of goaltender's skates will vary with the individual and often with the condition of the ice, as some ice rinks have harder or softer ice than others. The skates must be sharp enough to dig into the ice for powerful, explosive quick moves. Dull skates cannot do the job. Goal skates should have a less hollow ground than the skates of the forwards or defensemen.

At one time, goaltenders never touched the puck unless it was to prevent a goal. Modern goaltenders now play the puck anywhere in their area. Goaltenders now go behind the net to stop the puck and control the puck for a team-mate to pick up and start a play. Goaltenders now control the puck behind the net and in the corners to make the pass to set up the breakout. The goaltender passing the puck can be an excellent strategy as it saves time by not waiting for a team-mate to skate back to get the puck. Such a delay gives the opposition time to get organized. A good pass up the rink to a team-mate by the goaltender makes the attack much quicker and possibly more effective by catching the opposition off-guard. Effective goaltenders not only think of stopping the puck but plan on stopping the puck and organizing the attack or breakout.

A goaltender must use extreme caution when the opposition has control of the puck behind the goal net. At no time must you lose sight of the puck. The body must be positioned in relation to the puck. If the puck is on the left side behind the goal, the goalie should be positioned on the left post. When the puck moves to the right it is best to wait until the puck is halfway across the back of the net and then move to the right post. If the move is too soon, the puck carrier is able to change directions and slip back around the net and put the puck into the net in the spot just vacated by the goaltender.

When clearing or deflecting the puck, always clear against the direction of the attacking or shooting player. This type of clearing prevents the puck from being cleared or deflected to the attacker or shooter's direction of travel. If possible, clear and deflect to an open team-mate. Diagram 3-6 shows how the goaltender should clear the puck in direction B. If the goaltender clears the puck in direction A then the puck is cleared favorably to the attacker who just continues after the puck.

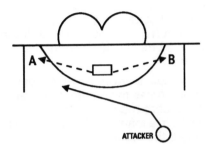

Diagram 3-6

Teammates Helping the Goaltender

Players must be careful when falling on their goaltender to help protect the puck. Falling on the goaltender very often does not protect the puck. Instead it hampers and restricts the movements of the goaltender. Sometimes falling on the goaltender dislodges the puck into the goal net. Instead of falling on the goaltender, the teammate should fall behind the goaltender to prevent a loose puck from slipping into the goal. Usually it is best to leave the goaltender alone. In the excitement of the situation, players fall on the goaltender to help him even though they do not see the puck. The goaltender's team-mates should not move to help the goaltender until they are sure of their actions or see the puck so they know where and what to protect.

Team-mates, especially the defensemen, must be careful when backing up towards the goal. The defensemen must shade to the side of a line from the puck to the center of the goal net. Some back-up to the goal post. The main purpose is to not block the vision of the goaltender. The goaltender is playing the puck, so he must be able to see it.

Team-mates must also use caution when trying to stop a shot on goal. If the shot is not fully stopped, a deflection may result. Deflected shots are a nightmare to the goalie. Often the goaltender is in position or moving to position to play the puck, only to be caught off-guard by a deflected puck.

Goaltender Helping his Teammates

Goaltenders should help their team-mates by yelling comments. Things like. "man behind you" or "far wing open" can be helpful to a team-mate. If a team-mate is blocking the vision of the goaltender the goaltender should not hesitate to yell for him to get out of the way. As goaltenders often have a good view of the rink and the developing patterns of play, he can often yell at his team-mates as to where to pass the puck.

Goaltenders can help their team-mates by stopping the puck behind the goal net. Sometimes the goaltenders can even control the puck and pass to a team-mate. Goaltenders should also be ready to receive a pass from a team-mate. As previously explained, goaltenders can originate the break-out play.

Goaltender Drills

In executing the drills, the goaltender must not only practice the proper execution but must also practice his orientation with the goal net. In the excitement of the action, it is easy to forget position and orientation. A few shots and the goaltender may end up way off line with the puck and the center of the goal. Coaches must continually monitor their goaltenders and provide opportunities for development of their positional play.

GOALTENDER DRILLS WITH NO PUCK

Post to post. The goaltender stands at one post and moves to the other post as fast as possible. The move is performed with only one push by the thrusting leg. While the body is moving from post to post, the upper body of the goaltender should remain square to the front of the net and an imaginary puck. The head must look forward and not to the post.

From front of the net and back to goal post. The goaltender stands in front of the goal net, usually just outside the crease. From this position, the goaltender backs into the net to the inside of the goal post, them moves back to the spot and backs up to the inside of the other goal posts. The goaltender continuously repeats the drill. At no time does the goaltender look for the goal posts. The body remains facing forward

Breaking in a pair of skates is usually an unwelcome duty. Leather skates are often more difficult but the process can be speeded by wetting the socks and then wearing the skates. Some players simply soak the new skates in water, lace them up and wear them for practice. With the plastic skate the fit of the skate at purchase is vital as the plastic skate will not mold to the foot like the leather boot.

A hockey player must take very good care of his skates. The blades should be wiped clean and dry after each use. If the blade and sides of the skate blade is allowed to rust the rusting action eats at the steel and can result in a poor edge when sharpened. Care should be taken when walking in skates to prevent nicks and dullness to the blade. Entrances to the ice and dressing room should be kept clean and free of anything that can dull or damage the skate blade edge. The skate blade edge is the only thing that gives the player contact with the ice. The blade must be sharpened expertly and must not be damaged by careless walking or unclean surfaces.

Hockey Sticks

Hockey sticks are usually a major expense. The coach should be familiar with the different companies and their price ranges. He should order a good stick that will serve the players and the budget. A hockey stick becomes a very personal item to a player. He trusts his stick and he has confidence in his hockey stick. A poor quality stick that does not meet the demands of the team can give the players a loss of confidence and low team moral. Some companies will even put the team name on the hockey stick and color the stick to the team's colors. Goal sticks are also expensive. Some goal sticks hold up better than others so care should be taken when ordering such sticks.

Supporter and Protective Cup

These items are required and easily purchased. Goalies have their own style of large protection. Most of these items are very similar. It is usually a question of what ones hold up the best over time.

Garter Belt

Like the supporters, poor quality garter belts will easily tear and wear and become unserviceable. It is often worth a few extra dollars for a better constructed garter belt.

Shin Pads

The coach should order good quality shin pads that provide excellent protection to the front of the shins and knees and to the side of the leg. The protective padding should not be bulky or cumbersome. The length of the pad is important for proper fitting on the leg of the player.

Elbow Pads

Elbow pads are important to the player. Some pads are too bulky and awkward. The size of the pad will depend on the size of the player.

Shoulder Pads

Like the elbow pads, the size and expense of the shoulder pads will vary according to the age, size and ability of the players. Usually the forward's style is smaller and lighter than the defensemen's pads with the extra chest and arm protection.

Chest Protectors

This is a goaltender item. The protector must be a good fit, light and yet not cumbersome. Despite these qualities it must offer excellent protection as the goaltender will be tested with many shots to the chest area. If the protector does not provide maximum protection the goaltender may develop a fear of shots to the chest. This is one item where the best is needed.

Hockey Pants

Hockey pants are designed to protect the vulnerable areas of kidneys, coccyx (tail bone), hips and thighs. Pants should be checked to be sure they do give the best protection possible. Try not to order pants that are too big for the players. If the pants are too large for the player the protective padding shifts around the player and may not be in the correct position when contact is made. A thigh pad that does not hug the thigh may shift off the thigh during a body check and leave the player with a severe injury. Pants with the tapered leg usually better hold the thigh pad in place. Hockey pants that do not fit snug may be risky to wear. Some companies now have the player's protective pads in the form of underwear so that the protective pads are held close to the body and in place. The hockey pant is a shell. The hockey pant shell with the underwear type pads is usually the best style of pant protection to purchase.

Hockey Gloves

The main emphasis in purchasing hockey gloves is the dexterity and manipulative factors along with protection. Not only do the hands need maximum protection but the protection must not hinder the agility of the hands. Good gloves usually meet these requirements, however, the gloves should be checked thoroughly. The palms of the glove are often the deciding factor on feel of the glove. Hockey gloves take a beating so be sure they are well constructed.

The goaltender's blocker and catching glove also become a very personal item to the goaltender. Very often it is best to let the goaltender pick out the model that will fit and feel best to him. Also, be aware when ordering to stipulate the need of the left handed or right handed combinations.

Helmets

Helmets are an essential piece of equipment. The fit should be snug. A loose helmet will slide around on contact or even slip off and leave the head vulnerable on contact. Protection cannot be provided with a helmet that will not stay in place to protect the area it is designed to protect. In selecting the helmet, pick a helmet with a chin strap that is easy to tighten, loosen, snap and unsnap. It is very annoying to a player when he has trouble with his chin strap.

Goal Masks

The mask is a very personal item. The goaltender must have a mask that is a perfect fit. He must have confidence in his mask. A mask that does not fit well is not only a nuisance, but it also may be dangerous. It is usually best to let the goaltender pick his mask.

Goal Leg Pads

In most cases, the top line or close to the top line goal pad is best for protection and upkeep. Good goal pads hold up to the demands of play. They maintain their shape longer and last longer before wearing out. Minor repairs may regularly be needed, but this is normal. Make minor repairs immediately before the damage turns into a major repair.

Mouthguards

Mouthguards are an inexpensive item and certainly are much cheaper than dental bills. Some mouthguards can be fitted by a dentist while other can be molded to the teeth by the individual himself. Some models are boiled in water and then the player bites into the mouthguard for a molded fit.

Equipment Bags

Equipment bags are made of various materials like canvas and vinyl. Usually the canvas style is best as there is a little breathing quality to the canvas. Vinyl does not breath and moisture inside the bag usually stays inside the bag. Hockey equipment is often packed slightly damp or even wet, so a little breathing quality can be helpful. Probably the most important feature in ordering bags is to be sure the size is large enough and that the goaltenders get the larger goaltender model. Be sure the stitching is strong. Check the carrying straps to be sure the straps are securely fastened to the bag. The straps should be designed so that the weight of the bag is evenly distributed through the straps. The suitcase style is easier to carry, pack and handle than the other styles like the duffle bag.

V. Injuries and Medical Problems

Injuries will occur even though excellent preventive measures are taken. A competent coach must know how to handle the injury when it occurs. He should know a little first aid but he must also be aware of his own limitations and responsibilities. In most instances, medical help should be used. Consulting a doctor will often take the burden of responsibility off the coach and transfer it to one who is qualified to diagnose and treat the injury. The coach must always remember that he is a coach and not a doctor.

Injuries and medical problems should be considered from four points of view: prevention, diagnosis, treatment and rehabilitation.

Prevention

Strength and flexibility of the athlete are strong factors in preventing an injury. The poorly conditioned athlete puts his muscles in an overtaxed state and thus becomes highly susceptible to strains and sprains. The more an athlete forces his muscles to go beyond his strength and flexibility level, the greater the possible seriousness of the injury. Therefore, the higher the strength and flexibility level the athlete can achieve, the less chance for injury.

Participation in sports requires energy. Since energy comes from food, the athlete must eat a balanced diet. Such a diet should include proteins, fats, carbohydrates, vitamins, minerals and water in proper proportions. A good diet will eliminate the need for pills and vitamins. The basic athletic diet consists mostly of carbohydrates for energy. The proteins repair torn tissue and the fats do provide some energy but not as quickly as the carbohydrates. The body requires about 60 -70% carbohydrates, 20 - 30% fats and 10 - 20% proteins. A coach in youth hockey will have little chance to influence the diets of the players. About all he can do is make his players aware of eating properly and hope the parents will help.

An athlete who has been eating well and regularity will be more alert and ready to participate in activity without undue fatigue. The athlete who tires easily because of poor diet, inadequate rest or poor conditioning makes himself a high risk for injury.

Equipment is very important in the prevention of injuries. A player must be adequately protected with properly fitted equipment. A player should not have to assume the risk of injury because of poor equipment.

Good coaching can also help to prevent injuries. Such things as proper line changes during a game help to prevent the tired player from over taxing his muscles. Progressive development of the player's skills will also help the player play correctly and more safely. Good officiating is another factor in injury prevention as the officials can keep the game under control and stop play as danger and illegal tactics develop.

It should be mandatory for all athletes to have a medical examination before being eligible to play or practice. The coach, school athletic director, or the team organization should have a medical record of each player. The medical record will provide a doctor with the player's history in the event treatment is needed. An example of the necessity of a medical history is in the event a player is allergic to penicillin.

Diagnosis

Some injuries are simple and can be treated by a coach or trainer if the treatment is uncomplicated. In making a diagnosis, the coach must be aware that many injuries are complicated and seem obscure from immediate or first diagnosis. A good example of this is referred pain which is difficult to evaluate because it is distant from the actual sight of the injury. Some injuries are latent in that they do not show up until well after the injury has occurred. Medical attention within twenty-four hours will help in the diagnosis and treatment of the injury as well as prevent further damage or re-injury.

Basic Treatment

Primary rules in injury treatment are:

W = Wrap: wrap or compress the injury.

R = Rest: rest the affected part-immobilize if necessary.

E = Elevate: if possible the affected part should be raised slightly when resting.

C = Cold: all injuries should be treated with cold treatments.

If you take the first letter on each of the treatments, W, R, E, C, we get the work WREC as a means to help remember the treatment.

The application of cold will help to reduce swelling and pain in the injured area: cold treatments should be applied immediately to the injury to prevent swelling. At no time should heat be applied to an injury before the passage of a minimum of forty-eight hours, and such treatment should be given as recommended by a doctor. During this forty-eight hour period, cold treatments should be given for twenty minutes every four hours.

Cold treatments and cold packs are terms used in the application of cold to an injury. A wet towel wrapped around snow or ice will produce an excellent cold pack. A frozen, water soaked sponge will work very well. When applied, the frozen sponge will soon take on the contours of the injured area and give an excellent fit. Commercial cold packs are good for instant use and when away from the access to ice.

Treatment for Specific Injuries and Conditions

CONTUSIONS (BRUISES)

Cold treatments should be immediately applied with the basic treatment. The player, if allowed to continue playing, may need the bruise protected. If the bruise is fairly serious, immobilization may be in order. Heat should not be applied to the injury until forty-eight hours after the occurrence unless prescribed by a doctor.

STRAINS

A strain is an overstretching of a muscle, which cannot occur without a tearing of muscle fiber and bleeding of capillaries. Treatment involves the immediate application of cold with the basic treatment.

SPRAINS

Sprains entail an overstretching or tearing of a ligament. They are most common and potentially the most disabling injury in all sports. Ligaments are notoriously slow to heal: if undertreated, they will not heal and the only alternative is surgical repair or transplant. Blood circulation of the ligament is scant and the full recovery period is at least six weeks.

A first degree sprain is simple overstretching and may be treated according to the principles of basic treatment.

A second degree sprain is a partial tearing or separation on the ligament with associated damage to blood vessels, soft tissues and capillaries (bleeding). Sprains must be treated with early immobilization, as if it were a fracture and rehabilitated gradually with supportive strapping for four to six weeks. As in the treatment of all sprains, immediate cold treatments are essential.

A third degree sprain is relatively rare. It is a complete division of the ligament, with all the neighboring damages, and should be corrected with an operation by a qualified specialist in bone and joint surgery.

It cannot be overemphasized that sprains occur at all ages in any part of the body and should not be neglected as they are by everyone who repeats the common fallacious expression, "It's only a sprain". It is very difficult, if not impossible, to immediately tell if the injury is a sprain or fracture. This is particularity true to the ankle injury. In most cases, an X-ray is needed.

WIND KNOCKED OUT

Tight clothing or equipment on the victim should be loosened. The victim will usually return to normal in a short period of time, but a check should be made for possible abdominal injuries resulting from the blow.

CRAMPS

The cramp is a muscle spasm caused by fatigue or diet deficiencies. If cramps persist with an individual then medical help may be needed. Cramps of an immediate nature can usually be cured be stretching and/or massaging of the muscle area. A short rest is also usually needed. For the side stitch cramp, rest is the usual cure.

CHARLEY HORSE

The charley horse injury is a muscle spasm common to the thigh or calf region. It may be due to any type of muscle damage - bruising, tearing, or abnormal circulation and metabolism. Initial treatment involves stretching the muscle to the point of fatigue so that it relaxes the knot, compressing the injury firmly, icing it, and then resting it. Subsequent treatment should be similar to that for a severe bruise. The charley horse should never be worked out by running, skating or massage. This working out treatment could be quite dangerous since severe damage can be inflicted to the muscle.

FRACTURES

If a bone break is suspected, the victim should not be moved until the injured area is splinted. The new air-inflatable splints can be easily and quickly applied. The player should be carefully placed on a stretcher and slid along the ice to the door. When off the ice, the victim may be lifted since the stretcher carriers will be able to obtain good footing. Cold packs should be immediately applied and medical help should be sought at once.

JOINT INJURIES

There are many types of joint injuries. They include the bruises and sprains on the ligaments of the joint, the strained muscle, fractures, and the bruised, torn or shattered cartilages of the joint.

The treatment for joint injuries is the basic treatment. It is vital to keep the knee and ankle from bearing weight until diagnosis by a doctor. The shoulder joint requires a sling to keep it immobilized. Separation and dislocation are the most common type of shoulder injuries. For the elbow, hyperextension is common.

HEAD INJURIES

A head injury may include external or internal bruising, or a skull fracture. The result can be partial or full loss of consciousness. Whenever a player is hit on the head, even if it looks minor at the time, keep him under close observation. In necessary, substitute for him and give him an immediate check-up. Look for signs of irregularity in his movement or mannerisms. Dilation of the eyes, poor vision, blurred sight and lack of parallelism of the eyes may be present. Sometimes a gawky expression will be noticeable. Dizziness, vomiting or convulsions may occur immediately or many hours later. Blood in the ears and nose is a sign of a severe head injury.

If any doubt exists call a doctor. The athlete should be under observation for the remainder of the day and night as well as for the next couple of days. If the boy lives at home, the parents should be instructed to maintain this observation. If the parents are not available, then a responsible person who is a room-mate or friend should have this duty. If an irregularity occurs during the night or the next day, a doctor must be notified. The irregularities may be vomiting, headache, dizziness, change of pulse rate or prolonged sleep. If the victim sleeps more than ten hours, he should be awakened and checked. If he does not awaken, the doctor is needed immediately. Quite often X-rays are required in evaluating the extent of injury.

If the victim suffers from immediate loss of consciousness, he should be transported on a stretcher to the dressing room or training room. The victim's head should be raised slightly higher than his feet. He should be kept warm and quiet in calm surroundings. An ice pack at the back of the neck or forehead is usually applied until the doctor arrives.

A player who is knocked unconscious but recovers should not be allowed to play for the remainder of the game, unless positive medical authority permits it.

A head injury is not necessarily a concussion. Concussion (an overused and misleading term) is the diagnosis made after recovery to denote a head injury with no serious after-effects.

FACIAL INJURIES

Bruises are a common type of facial injury. Immediate cold treatments are essential. Bruise treatment was discussed earlier in this chapter. Contusions are a bruise and should be treated accordingly.

A black eye is a type of bruise. In itself it is usually harmless, but it may be a sign of a more severe injury. Since a blow is usually the cause of this injury, one should look for damage to the eye, nose and skull. A black eye is often associated with a fracture. It is also necessary to check the eyeball itself; a medical opinion is essential in this situation. No player should participate without good vision, since the player becomes very susceptible to injury. A cold pack applied to the eye area will help to slow down the hemorrhaging (the discoloration is the result of minute vessels, which are broken and are bleeding under the skin).

Jaw injuries such as broken jaws are commonly caused by cross-checking and high-sticking. Usually the victim will suffer pain when yawning and chewing. A medical diagnosis is essential to treatment.

With a broken nose, swelling will immediately take place. There will be some deformity, pain and bleeding. Sometimes the blow may cause one or two black eyes. The athlete must breathe through his mouth; the nose should not be blown or squeezed. An absorbent pad to catch the blood should be placed lightly over the bleeding area. Ice packs are necessary in slowing down the bleeding and swelling. A doctor should be consulted.

For a nose bleed, a cold pack should be applied to the nose and back of the neck. The patient should be sitting up with his head back. Gauze pads or cotton batting should be held at the nostril. If bleeding cannot be stopped, then medical help may be needed. Sometimes the nose is bruised to the extent that it causes bleeding into the septum (middle of the nose). This necessitates medical treatment, since it may lead to permanent injury and difficulty in breathing.

NECK AND SPINAL INJURIES

Neck and spine injuries encompass a wide range. Most are mild, but they can have serious consequences. The majority of such injuries are not noticed until after the game or on the next day. The coach must be alert for them.

If a player lying on the ice complains of pain in the spinal region, then no attempt should be made to move him until a doctor or highly qualified first-aid people arrive and are able to direct the procedure. If necessary, the players may have to return to the dressing room and wait until the injured player is properly removed.

A good rule to follow is: Do not move the player, ask him to move. If he cannot, then presume there is a serious injury.

OPEN WOUNDS AND ABRASIONS

The wound should be cleansed and any foreign bodies removed. A germicide should be used to help kill germs and prevent infection. A first-aid cream will also be helpful. If possible, the wound should be exposed to the air to heal faster; otherwise a bandage will be necessary.

BLISTERS

A blister is caused by friction or pressure on the foot within the boot. To prevent further pressure or friction, a felt pad with a hole cut, a little larger than the blister, should be fastened to the foot so that the blister sits in the hole of the pad. If liquid is in the blister, it can be drained by puncturing the skin at the edge of the blister, although this is a controversial procedure due to the possibility of infection. If a blister is open it is treated as an open wound. Improper care and treatment can very easily result in infection.

BLOW TO THE SCROTUM

Even with the use of a protective cup, this injury is still possible. To relieve pain, the athlete should lie on his back with his legs bent. Tight clothing should be loosened although it is unlikely the player will be wearing anything tight. Pain will usually subside in a few minutes. After this injury, the player should be checked for swelling, for pain in the area, or for a missing testicle (pushed up) before returning to play. If any of these symptoms are present a doctor is essential.

ATHLETE'S FOOT

Athlete's foot is a skin disorder due to a fungus. Prevention is the best treatment. Floors should be kept dry and disinfected and showers should be clean and sanitary at all times. The feet should be dried thoroughly and socks changed daily. White socks aid in the cleanliness of the feet. A foot powder or cream will aid in fighting this disease. It becomes an extreme problem to the team or individual then medical help will be needed.

JOCK STRAP RASH

Most jock strap rashes are due to inflammations of the skin due to chemical burns, infections or friction rubs. The rash is best treated by keeping the rash area clean and dry without the use of strong soaps, detergents or other chemicals. Some rashes will respond to exposure of first-aid creams or powders. If there is not rapid progress in healing, medical diagnosis and treatment should be sought.

TEETH INJURIES

Teeth injuries should be immediately referred to a dentist.

Rehabilitation

The rehabilitation of injuries is the most crucial consideration in their management and it requires experienced judgment and knowledge of the activity in which the person is to participate. The coach and medical staff should consult closely in gradually re-conditioning the treated athlete to maximum fitness before permitting full participation. Special protective strapping, padding or guards may assist in the early return to a full performance.

Some Basic Guidelines

Whenever there is a chance of injury, physical or mental harm and the need for first-aid, a coach must be aware of liability problems. The following guidelines may be of help in preventing liability law suites.

REMAIN CALM

Remain calm so that you can present an image of being in control. By being calm, the thought process can be organized and accurate. Anxiety and pressure affect not only the players but also the coach.

NEVER ASSUME THE ROLE OF A PHYSICIAN

Put the responsibility of diagnosis on the physician who is qualified to make such decisions. Unless you are a doctor you haven't been trained to diagnose medical problems.

NEVER DO ANYTHING THAT COULD BE INTERPRETED AS GROSS NEGLIGENCE

Remember, as a coach you have assumed responsibility for the care of your players. Do not be negligent. Supervise all activities.

NEVER MOVE A PLAYER WITH A SUSPECTED SERIOUS IN-JURY

This means not sitting him up, rolling him over, straightening the legs, etc. Leave the movement to qualified people.

DO NOT TAKE CHANCES WITH THE HOPE NOTHING MAY HAPPEN.

Use good judgement making decisions.

DO NOT PLAY THE GAME IF SERIOUS INJURY IS POSSIBLE TO A PLAYER OR TEAM.

Safety is a must. Regularity inspect equipment and facilities.

NEVER PLAY A PLAYER AFTER A SERIOUS INJURY OR SUS-PECTED SERIOUS INJURY.

Some injuries are latent and take effect after the incident. Sometimes the extra physical effort after an injury will magnify the injury to permanent damage. Head injuries have caused death while playing well after the incident.

VI. Coaching Duties

Coaching is a year-round job. The off-season should be used to formulate plans and organize for the upcoming season. Beginning the season in an orderly manner will enhance a smooth progression from the off-season, to the pre-season, to the season. Good organization will give the players a feeling of confidence with the coach and management. Disruptions will occur, but the well prepared coach will be ready to meet these disruptions. A coach, when planning, should always plan for "Murphy's Law," whatever can go wrong will. A coach that plans for these problems will be prepared for them if they occur. This type of coach is a well prepared coach.

Pre-Season Arrangements

Arrangements for facilities, equipment and training should be made before the season starts. Many of these things will be done during the off-season. If they are done during the off-season, then they should be checked and verified during the pre-season so that all systems are go for the season.

Practice Planning

GOALS AND OBJECTIVES

Practice planning is a combination of long-term goals and short-term goals. The coach must develop his long-term goals from his philosophy of the game. His desired style of play for the future is part of the long-term goal. His short-term goals lead up to his long-term plans and his philosophy. This planning takes time and should not be treated lightly. Plan so you know where you are going and how you are going to get there.

REPETITION

We practice our skills over and over until we have improved or mastered them. Repetition, at least correct repetition, seems to be a key factor in learning and retaining our skills. Learning skills requires time, lots of time. The coach must give adequate time to learning, retaining and refining the skills of the game. The coach's practice planning must reflect this time requirement.

GAME CONDITIONS

Drills and practice planning should be designed from and reflect game conditions. How the coach wants it done during a game is the way it should be practiced. If the game plan is for short passes then the practice should be planned around the short passing game.

Fundamentals must still be emphasized with all drills. Game strategy is important but it must not neglect the fundamentals. Poor fundamentals in skating, puck control and goaltending will result in poor game strategy. Fundamentals are the basis of all sports and the kids must learn this in the youth programs. *Youth programs are about developing players, not won-loss records*.

DRESSING ROOM TALKS

To save ice time, the coach should do his talking and explaining in the dressing room before going on the ice. A chalk board or any other type of visual aid can be used to explain the practice and drill to the players. This means ice time is saved. Long discussions on the ice is dead time. Sometimes discussions on the ice are needed, but if ice time is expensive and your budget is tight, then keep the on-ice practice moving and do the long talks in the dressing room.

TEAM MEETINGS

Team meetings can be helpful to the players and coach if properly handled. The meetings should be short and fun. If team strategy is discussed, keep it simple, short and effective. Previously videotaped games or practices can be effective with care and planning. Besides, kids love to see themselves playing on video. If the video is used for analysis then keep the analysis to a few key points. Do not overload the youngsters head with facts and information. Good youth coaches do not try to impress the kids with there knowledge. Good coaches teach.

DEMONSTRATIONS

In most cases, the coach should have his players demonstrate. This gives recognition to the player and helps with the confidence of his players. With the players demonstrating, the coach is free to comment on technique and point out the key points. As a coach gets older his demonstrations may not be as good as he thinks. Some demonstrations seem to be a means of "showing off." Be careful not let this happen to you. Some coaches demonstrate because they do not know how to adequately comment on the technique. They know how to do the skill, but they do not know how to teach it. Another important consideration in demonstrations is that when one demonstrates, the observers or players will focus on the results of the demonstration and not on the technique of the skill. For example, if the coach is demonstrating the slap shot, the players will focus on how accurate or powerful his shot is and not on the technique. To help the players focus on the technique, the coach must tell the players what to look for. Slow motion demonstrations can help focus on a certain part of the skill. Also, just going through the motion without shooting the puck can be helpful.

When using the demonstration technique, coaches must be careful not to talk too much. A good demonstration can be ruined by talking too much. Youngsters have short attention spans and want to move on to new adventures after a short period of time. Talking should emphasis the key points quickly and precisely. Kids have amazing abilities to imitate, so the players are using visual learning skills with little audio attention.

VARIETY AND INTEREST

Practice sessions need variety and interest, and the coach should not let the practices become routine or stereotyped. Usually there are many drills that can accomplish the same purpose so it is advisable to vary the drills to help maintain interest. With this in mind, the coach should be careful to not overuse a drill so that it becomes boring. Boring drills lead to carelessness in execution.

Plan around the short attention span of the age group. The drills have to be very simple for the very young groups as their attention and skill is very poor. As players get older their attention spans increase and the skill level also improves. As players become more advanced, the drills and practices must also advance in complexity so as to maintain interest with the players. If the skill level is too high for some of the simple drills, the players will also get bored and dissatisfied. Hockey players develop very rapidly every year. Coaches must plan and practice with this development in mind. Otherwise the players will become bored by the lack of challenge or confused by complexity. Plan your strategy around your team's abilities.

EVALUATION

It is a good idea for the coach to keep his practice plans for evaluation. For example, if a coach discovers that his breakout play is not working, he can check his plans for time allotment on the breakout play. If the check reveals that insufficient time was spent on the breakout play, then future practices can be adjusted accordingly. If sufficient time was given to the breakout play, then the coach must decide why it is not working. Perhaps the learning situation was not good; maybe the coaching was inadequate;

maybe the style of teaching did not working with this group; or maybe the players are slow learners. These are difficult questions to answer. It is not easy to say the coaching was weak, despite all the work and effort that went into the practices. At times, work and effort are not enough, results are what count. Evaluate and correct your errors honestly.

FLEXIBILITY AND CHANGES

The practice plans should remain flexible. If some phases are not progressing as fast as predicted, then future sessions have to be adjusted to meet this demand. The plan for the day, however, should usually remain the same. Adjustments are for the next day. Too many last minute adjustments will throw off the overall plan. If 15 minutes are allowed for penalty killing and success is not achieved in that time, then move on to the next drill and adjust the plan for the next practice and succeeding practices. This prevents a coach from failing to practice an important phase of the game, and will allow time after the practice to better analyze the situation for corrections.

The coach should outline what he wants to develop for the season. This season plan is then broken down into smaller units, perhaps weekly or bi-weekly. The units are then broken down into the individual practice sessions.

Sample Practice Plan

Plan for the week: emphasize puck control.

Monday	2 hours	Thursday	2 hours
Tuesday	2 hours	Friday	2 hours
Wednesday	2 hours	Saturday	2 hours

Total   12 hours/720 minutes

Breakdown for the week: 12 hours = 720 minutes

GAME PHASE

Skating (100 minutes)

forward	20 min.
backward	40
lateral	40

Puck control (300 minutes)

stickhandling	100
passing/ receiving	100
shooting	100

Offense (120 minutes)

basic attack	60
breakout	60

Defense (120 minutes)

forechecking	60
stickchecking	30
backchecking	30

Situations (60 minutes)

one-on-one	15
two-on-one	15
two-on-two	15
three-on-two	15

Total time allotted for the week: 720 minutes

Total time planned for the week: 700

Time left over for cushion: 20

Daily Practice: Monday

Time Drill

2:40   Meeting, orientation for practice. Be dressed at this time.

2:50   Free time on ice.

3:00   Skating (10 minutes)

1 min. - forward laps
1 min. - breaking between blue lines
1 min. - breaking around corners
1 min. - backward laps
1 min. - figure eight
3 min. - lateral stationary side to side
2 min. - mirror drill

3:10   Puck control (50 minutes)

        3 min. - stickhandling laps
        3 min. - figure eight
        4 min. - right/left carry
        2 min. - sweep to each side
        3 min. - breaking at blue line
        4 min. - passing stationary 20 feet apart
        4 min. - stationary backhand
        9 min. - give and take
     10 min. - shooting slap shot inside blue line
        5 min. - deking and fake shot
        4 min. - flip shot from red line

4:00   Offense (20 minutes)

        4 min. - drop pass on blue line
        4 min. - dack pass to blue line
     12 min. - back pass to partner and shoot

4:20   Defense (20 minutes)

     10 min. - forechecking in corner
        5 min. - stickchecking partners
        5 min. - backchecking

4:40   Situations (10 minutes)

        5 min. - one-on-one
        5 min. - two-on-one

4:50   Skating (8 minutes)

        2 min. - stop and start on whistle
        2 min. - length of ice
        2 min. - backward agility
        2 min. - scooting

4:58   Cool down

Sample Check List

The check list is an excellent means of recording how much time is spent on each phase of the game. All possible skills or situations are listed down the side of a sheet of paper. The minutes are recorded under the date column. The coach can evaluate his time allotments as the season progresses.

Month: November

SESSION

SKILL	1	2	3	4	5	6	7
conditioning	10	5	10	15			
skating	15	15	10	15			
stickhandling	10	15	5	15			
passing	20	15	20	10			
shooting	10	15	10	15			
checking	5	15	5	15			
individual skills							
defensemen	10	10	10				
forwards	10	10	10				
offense	20	20	15				
defense							
face-offs			5	5			
penalty killing							
power play							
pulled goalie	15						
line changes	10						
delayed penalty							
broken stick	5						
TOTAL	120	120	115	90			

Discipline

A hockey technique should never be used as a disciplinary measure. Many coaches use extra skating or stop-and-start drills as a form of punishment. This form of punishment uses a desired result in a negative situation. Hard skating is what a coach needs in his players, therfore hard skating should be a reward and not a punishment. Extra laps given in fun or for conditioning are not only beneficial but can help boost team morale. Discipline problems are usually best handled off the ice.

Importance of Understanding the Athlete

The coach should gain as much knowledge about his players as possible. He is working with human beings, not robots. A knowledge of his player's backgrounds, attitudes and desires will help the coach understand his players. Knowing and helping his players is a year-round job.

As players move up in age and league status, the competition becomes keener and tougher. The better players remain and the poorer players drop out. First year players who have just moved up to a higher calibre of play must adjust, not only to the higher level of play but also to the different social level of the team. Some players can handle the playing level but have problems with the new team environment and different players. Some players were stars at the lower level and now must cope with the situation of being an average or even a below average player in the higher league. This can be a tremendous psychological strain on the player. Such players may lose confidence and may even desire to quit the team. The coach must be aware of these types of problems and make every effort to prevent the collapse of a player. Patience, understanding and guidance can help some players. Coaches must recognize potential or possible potential and help the player. The coach will not always be successful but it is worth a try.

Personal Contact

The importance of personal contact with the players must be fully realized by the coach. The coach should always be with his team when they are together. If he is absent, the players may feel the coach has let them down, or the occasion is not important. During game situations, the coach should be in the dressing room to meet the arrival of the players. By being the first on the scene, the coach may be able to set the tone and atmosphere before the game. The coach should also be with the team between periods to set a tone provide guidance for the next period. After the players have settled down, the coach will be able to discuss plans and answer questions.

Personal contact is especially important with youth players. With older players in the college and pro ranks it is not as important, but to the youth player the coach is extremely important. The coach is a role model to the players in many ways. Being a role model puts a lot of pressure on the coach. Expectations are very high. Youth coaching is extremely difficult because knowledge of just hockey skills is not enough. In fact, your knowledge of the game is less important than the example you set for the players.

Coaching Uniform

Dress properly. Always be warm. Nothing can be more annoying than being slightly cold during practice or a game. Usually, it is best to have some kind of uniform for practice. A sweat suit is most common and serves quite well. Some may like to wear jacket and pants. Some like a sweater instead of a jacket. By wearing a special uniform the players sense you are serious about your job. A coaching uniform shows activity, the coach is active and involved.

Managers

The selection of a manager is extremely important. He is a key person and is as valuable as any player. The manager is valuable for team moral. A good, happy manager can help instill the same attitude with the team. A manager is a link between the player and the coach and his understanding of the players can be an asset to the coach. The manager must be loyal, trustworthy and dependable. If he cannot meet these demands then dismissal may be appropriate. The manager must be available when the players need him. Often the manager may be required for minor injuries and first-aid unless a trainer is with the team. If the team has more than one manager, then each manager must have his duties defined so that there is no overlap of functions or confusion of tasks. Good managers often go unnoticed despite the fact that the smooth operation of the team may depend on them. A wise coach will make his manager very aware of his contribution to the team.

At the youth level, some coaches like to have an adult or even one of the parents as manager. Some coaches like to give this responsibility to a kid at the same age level as the players. There are good and bad reasons for each selection. The coach should evaluate the team's needs and what will work best for it. The manager is an important selection so choose accordingly.

Team Captains

The team captain or captains are appointed or elected. The choice is up to the coach. The captain is the liaison between the players and the coach. The responsibility given to the captain is dependent on the coach. Some captains are given duties and responsibilities while some are only figureheads. There are advantages and disadvantages as to whether the captains are elected or appointed, with duties or no duties. The coach must evaluate his situation.

Legal Liability

A coach must always be aware of legal liability. If uninsured, he may want to protect himself with insurance. The following rules may be helpful.

1. Never leave your players unsupervised.

2. Know first-aid, but never take on the duties of a doctor.

3. Do not let a player run the risk of injury through negligence. The safety and care of the players is the coach's responsibility.

4. Try to have a doctor at all home games and practices.

5. Never give pep pills or any type of drugs to the players. Leave this to the doctor. Do not even give over the counter drugs like

aspirin.

6. Do not allow anyone to participate without a medical examination or parental approval.

7. Make all recommendations for safety measures in writing to your superiors and make a photocopy. Keep one copy and send the other to the league, school, owner, or whoever is responsible.

8. Insist on hygiene and safety at all times.

Recommendations for hygiene would be showers, clean equipment, clean dressing rooms, etc. Each player must hang up his own equipment and put waste, tape, etc., in the refuse can. There should be no throwing of tape, snow from the skates, or anything that may be dangerous to the eyes. If the dressing room is only used for the practice or game, then the players and coach should leave the room clear of refuse and waste material.

Slumps or Staleness

Staleness results when no learning takes place. The coach should always try to keep a learning situation in the daily practices. Sometimes the slumps occur when preventative measures are taken. Usually, if an athlete is giving an all out effort all the time, he is susceptible to a slump. If an athlete never has a slump, then he may be suspect of not giving his all. Staleness may be suffered by an individual or the team. Staleness to the individual may not be as disastrous as staleness to the team. Various tactics may be successful. Which one will work is never known until it is tried. Some of the tactics are to check a player's technique. A change in routine may help. An increase in the work load has proven helpful. Short practice sessions and canceled practices often help.

Player Development

The coach should be concerned with the development of future players. The success of the higher level teams depends on the progression of younger talent. In most cases, the success of a high school team is a result of the quality of the youth program in the school district. The high school coach and higher level coach should always take an interest and, if possible, help with the youth programs. The youngsters appreciate this and will look forward to playing for such a coach. In many cases, some players are not quite ready for the higher level because of their age. Good coaches realize some players develop physically later than others and keep them on the team for developmental purposes. The coach must recognize potential and give such players the chance and time to adjust and develop.

The Pre-game Warm-up

The following is an example of a pre-game warm-up that has been used with excellent results. The warm-up covers forward and backward skating, stickhandling, puck control, passing, receiving, shooting, offense and defense. The goaltender receives shots from all angles as well as game condition shots. This warm-up is diagramed under the drills chapter.

1. Each player carries a puck onto the ice. The signal for changing drills is given by the captain yelling or whistling.

2. The players skate and stickhandle in single file in a large circle on their half of the rink.

3. When the command is given, the players stop, reverse directions, skate and stickhandle in the other direction.

4. On another command, the players join with partners and skate around in their circle giving and receiving short passes.

5. On the command, the players position themselves on one side of the ice for the two-on-one drill. As the two-on-one unit finishes their attempt, the players position themselves on the other side of the ice for another two-on-one drill.

6. On the command, the centermen line up in the middle ice area with their wingers to each side along the boards. A defenseman in the corner passes out to the centerman who in turn passes to a breaking winger for a shot on goal. The centerman then receives another pass from the defenseman, passes to his other winger and then goes to the back of the centermen's line. The next centerman then takes his turn at passing to his wingers.

7. On the command, the players skate the circle backwards and follow their captain into the dressing room.

Between Periods of the Game

The coach should follow his team into the dressing room to get them settled and quiet. It is usually best to have the dressing room free of extra people. Only the coaches, players and managers need to be in the dressing room. Extra people are distractions to the task at hand.

The managers should have cold, wet towels and dry towels to pass around. Oranges, lemons and liquid drinks should be readily available. If the coach has to talk to someone not on the team, it is best to do so outside the dressing room.

After the team has settled down, they will be more receptive to criticism or praise. By waiting until the last half of the rest period the player's minds will have cleared and tactics can be better understood. The dressing room atmosphere is important to the players. The coach should maintain this atmosphere with his leadership.

After the Game

After the game there is nothing that will change the outcome of the game. The game is over. Severe criticism is best saved until the next practice or next day. By waiting a day, the coach gets more time to thoroughly evaluate the game and his criticism. Also, by waiting for the next day the players have time to settle down, be more receptive to criticism and have had a chance to look at themselves objectively. In many cases, the players know the criticism is coming so the extra time gives them preparation time. Severe criticism immediately after the game usually catches the players while they are exceptionally mad, charged up and excited. It is very easy for hard feelings to occur. Rash, impulsive statements after a hard fought battle can lead to bitter resentment among the players and between the coaches and players.

VII. Selecting the Team

One of the most difficult aspects of coaching is the selection of players for the team. Every player must be given a fair chance to display his talents. If a player is cut, he should be able to talk to the coach to find out why he did not make the team. Sometimes it is advisable to give the player another chance to prove himself. When the player has another chance he often gets a closer look for evaluation. Giving players a retry not only sets up a procedure of fairness, but it is especially fair when ice time is scarce and the tryout procedure is limited. At the beginning of the season, some players take time to adjust and get ready for the team. The coach must not be too quick to cut a player.

As an aid to selecting a team, the coach may find a rating system helpful. A rating system forces the coach to look at all the important features of a player. Often when the coach relies on just observation without notation, it is possible to miss an important aspect of a player. A rating system can help the coach in organizing this difficult task. There may be nothing worse than cutting a player because of a poor and inefficient evaluation system.

NAME	NO	SKATING	SHOOTING	PASSING	PASS RECEIVING	STICK HANDLING	HOCKEY SENSE	POTENTIAL	RATING	COMMENTS
WALLS	2	1	2	2	3	3	2	1	14	GOOD PROSPECT
JONES	3	5	2	4	5	4	5	4	32	NO CHANCE
DUNN	4	2	3	3	3	2	2	1	16	PROMISE

diagram 7-1

Diagram 7-1 is a sample chart of a rating system. A coach may modify this system to meet his needs. Each skill is rated on a scale of 1 to 5 with 1 as the top score. The overall rating is the total score with the lowest score being the best score. It is possible that some players may score poorly in the overall total but have some outstanding features or scores on some skills. These outstanding individual skill scores may give the coach cause for keeping a player, or at least taking another look. However the scores are used, they should not be the final criteria. The scores are only an aid to evaluation and selection.

Testing

In selecting a team, the coach may find that testing the players in certain game skills can be very helpful. The testing program is a guide and not the final criteria. Tests can help provide the coach with a look at the potential of the players. Players with excellent skill scores but not performing well in game conditions may have mental problems in adjusting to game conditions. If his skills are high then maybe a little help and time will develop the player's game strategy. Youth coaches must look for potential. Some players are late developers. They need a chance. Selecting a team and cutting players from the team is a tremendous responsibility.

The following is a hockey skills test, devised by the author for a M.Sc. degree requirement. The validity and reliability of this test is very high.

OVERALL PROCEDURES

1. All times are stopped when the first skate touches the finish line.
2. All times should be recorded to the nearest tenth of a second.
3. A performer is allowed two tries for each event with the best score counting.
4. All starts are from a motionless standing start.

Puck Carry Test (Diagram 7-2)

The puck is placed on the goal crease line and the player stands behind the line with his skates facing straight ahead and the feet side by side. The player must carry the puck to the end and back, while weaving around each obstacle. If the player loses the puck, his time continues as he recovers and resumes progress at the point of error. If two or more obstacles are knocked over, the score is disqualified and the run counts as an attempt.

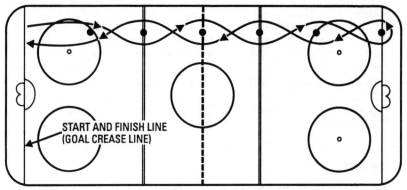

Diagram 7-2

Speed Forward Test (Diagram 7-3)

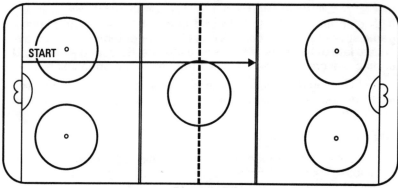

Diagram 7-3

The player starts behind the crease line with his feet side by side and facing straight ahead. The player skates as fast as possible to the second blue line. If the player falls, his time continues until he crosses the finish line.

Speed Backward Test

The speed backward test is the same as the speed forward test. The player starts from a motionless stand with his back to the finish line. The performer is not allowed to pivot to forward skating and back to backward skating in order to build up speed.

Agility Test (Diagram 7-4)

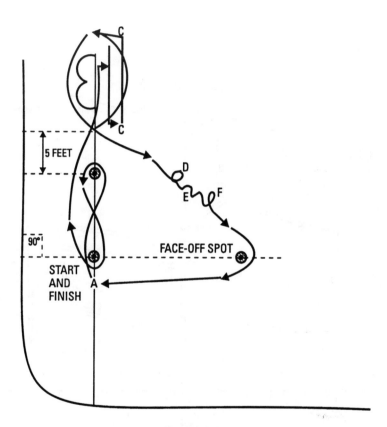

Diagram 7-4

The performer starts by straddling the goal crease line at 'A.' The hockey stick must be held below waist level at all times during the run. At 'C,' the performer must cross the goal crease line with both feet, stop and go. At 'D,' the player pivots to backward skating and then must take at least one backward stride at 'E,' and then return to forward skating at 'F.'

Shooting Tests (Diagram 7-5)

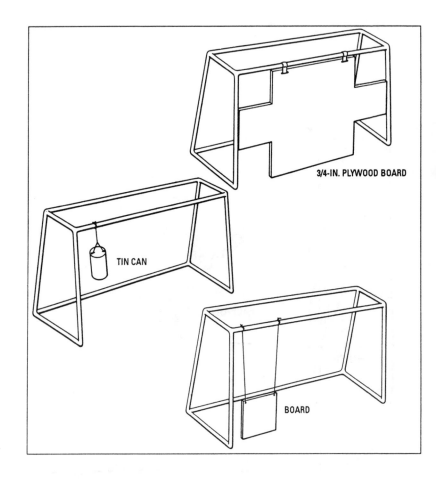

3/4-IN. PLYWOOD BOARD

TIN CAN

BOARD

Diagram 7-5

The shooting test does not have the high validity of the other four tests. Despite this fact, they can be used for evaluation. The players do enjoy doing these tests to see how they compare with each other.

Passing Test (Diagram 7-6)

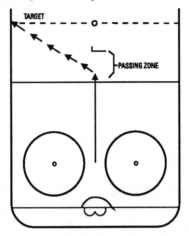

Diagram 7-6

The passing test is not as valid as the other test, but it does give some indication as to skill. A hockey stick is placed on the ice halfway between the red line and the blue line. The player skates towards the hockey stick and is required to make the pass between the stick and the blue line, while not stopping. In most cases, the blue line on the boards can be used as the target. If this is too small a target then make a larger one. The pass must be made with the puck sliding along the ice and not above the ice.

Testing Layout (Diagram 7-7)

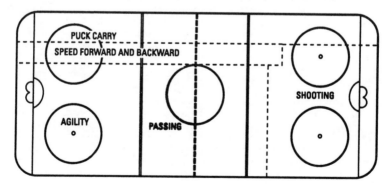

Diagram 7-7

The coach can administer each test himself or he can set up a rotational system, where all tests are done together with the players rotating from station to station. The rotational system requires more help, but it does get the testing done quicker. Some coaches prefer to administer one test at each practice as a fun-time session.

Another advantage of the testing program is for youth hockey programs. Some city youth programs have used the scores with tremendous success in selecting their teams. The scores are ranked in order. Then, going down the list, the players are assigned to teams. For example, a youth program with six teams would assign the players as follows:

TEAM A	TEAM B	TEAM C	TEAM D	TEAM E	TEAM F
1	2	3	4	5	6
12	11	10	9	8	7
13	14	15	16	17	18

Player Development

The coach should be concerned with the development of future players. The success of the higher level teams depends on the progression of younger talent. In most cases, the success of the high school team is a result of the quality of the youth program in the school district. Coaches above the youth leagues should always take an interest and help with the youth programs when possible. The youngsters appreciate it.

VIII. Fitness

This chapter contains information that can be beneficial to the coach and players. Maturity levels among the younger and older age groups varies. The following information must be broken down to the skill level and maturity level of the team. Some of the information is too advanced for the younger groups and some of the information may be too simple for the older age groups. The coach must utilize this information to his team's level.

Developing a Program

GOAL SETTING

To develop a conditioning program, the coach must set goals. These goals are for the team and each athlete. To set goals, the coach must know the ability and skill level of his players'. The plans must include short-term goals and long-term goals.

In business, the Management by Objectives (MBO) concept is highly effective for coaches. MBO means that by a certain date or time, certain objectives must be met or accomplished. Through the use of the game schedule, the coach plans for the season and off-season. The plans are designed to meet certain objectives by a certain date. The pre-season may include a heavy emphasis in aerobic conditioning. Next comes an emphasis in interval training and anaerobic demands for the remainder of the season. Mid-season may include a new attack strategy. The basic power play should be accomplished by the end of November with a new variation or style added each month. Naturally, the objectives will be more detailed than outlined here.

The biggest difficulty in planning is that often the plans lack realistic objectives. On paper, we sometimes think we accomplish things faster than we actually do. It is best to begin with simple and easy objectives. If things go faster than expected, we have some extra time. Also, psychologically we may feel a sense of accomplishment as each goal is achieved. This may be a motivational devise.

Implementing a training program requires knowledge of the conditioning process, as well as the game of hockey and the style of play. The coach must determine the style of play for the season and adapt the conditioning program to the demands of that style.

When coaching the younger age groups, the objectives will be very different from those of the older age groups. Perhaps a trend will show itself, such as a younger player needing more individual objectives, like learning to shoot the puck, stickhandling without looking at the puck, etc. As younger players advance to the upper age levels, the goals will become increasingly more oriented towards the team aspect. Another aspect of the younger age groups is that the goals and objectives will require more flexibility. It is difficult to evaluate the time frame for the young players. At times, they learn fast, while other times they seem to take longer. Be patient and have flexibility.

Interest and Motivation

An extremely important factor in designing the program is interest and motivation. Conditioning is painful and boring, but it is required and needed for any kind of team development. Plan for interest. Plan for fun. Never forget that interest and fun apply to all levels of ability – from youth to the pros. The pros like to have fun at practice just like kids. Humor is a strong part of the conditioning process. Kids want to have fun while working hard, so design your practices accordingly.

Game Conditions

The training program must be demanding and as close to game conditions as possible. Practices must condition not only the body, but also the mind. The mind learns to function and think under fatigue and stress. This is vital to performance. Practices must be kept moving. Dead time must be eliminated and talking must be at a minimum. Keep lectures and talk to a minimum when on the ice. Long talks are best before or after practice. During a game, the player is on the ice functioning under extreme body demands, and then rests before returning for his next shift.

Training programs must develop the cognitive or thinking required for actual games. An athlete will ease up, both mentally and physically when fatigued. As a coach, you must not allow this to happen. Hockey requires intelligent and quick thinking. Practices must be planned for the thought process as well as the physical aspect. Sometimes it may be beneficial to fatigue the athlete at the beginning of practice and then work on complex drills and positional play in order to help train the athlete to think correctly while fatigued.

Over-training

Over-training may be one of the most serious training problems affecting a team. No one knows can say for sure where the line between productive and counter productive practicing lies. Experience seems to be the best teacher. The coach must continually look for signs of overtraining. At times, it is beneficial to ask the players how they feel.

Quite often over-training is the result of a guilty conscience. The coach, and sometimes the players, feel for the need to practice and are afraid to take a day off or cut practice short. What makes over-training so difficult to cope with is the fact that most athletes suffer from it at different times. Over-training often leads to staleness. Staleness is a state of apathy, or lack of excitement. The athlete is bored with the routine. The coach must plan for staleness and be ready with counter measures when needed.

Boredom and staleness are the result of a lack of learning, or a lack of progression. Planning should try to introduce new ideas to provide variety. In athletics, we often learn everything before the season, and then practice it the rest of the season. When the team reaches the last half of the season, quite often nothing new is learned or practiced. Therefore, the last half of the season is susceptible to boredom and staleness.

Planning for staleness is difficult and not always possible to predict. But the coach can assume the possibilities of staleness will increase as the season progresses.Youngsters are particularly vulnerable to becoming bored. Coaches tend to find a good drill and work it to death in as they teach. Find new and different ways to teach learning skills. Keep things interesting and exciting. Little, if any, learning takes place when kids are just going through the motions of doing a drill. Continually find ways to challenge them.

Rest

An athlete requires rest. Exercise tears the body down. Rest rebuilds the body for the new demands placed on it. Lack of rest will gradually wear the body down to a point where it becomes inefficient. Fatigue becomes chronic or temporarily permanent. Prolonged fatigue is detrimental to the athlete's performance and may require a doctor's intervention. A restless night before a game is not necessarily a problem because many athletes do not sleep well the night before competition. The problem with lack of rest is in prolonged stages of days or weeks.

Sometimes too much rest is also detrimental to performance. Too much sleep makes the body lazy, not only physically but mentally. Road trips are often plagued by too much sleep. The athlete sleeps in late in the morning and then takes naps during the day because there is nothing else to do. By game time the athlete may be mentally foggy with slow reactions.

Ice time is often another problem. Some programs can only schedule ice time early in the morning or late at night. At the beginning of the season this practice time may not be a problem because the players are excited and ready to get started. As the season progresses, the players can slowly wear down under the strain. Be alert to this situation. Continually observe the players for signs of fatigue. If needed, a practice may have to be canceled or just have a fun practice.

Pace the Conditioning Process

The coach must pace the conditioning process during the season. The body needs to be sharp for special games and rested during certain periods of the season. Planning may help prevent being stale or flat for important games, especially late in the season. When planning for rest, through light activity, be careful that the situation does not breed carelessness in execution. When taking it easy, correct execution must be demanded while the energy demands are lessened.

Do not schedule heavy conditioning practices after demanding games, especially after two days of physically stressful games. Under this type of stress, the body needs rest to recover and rebuild its body tissues. A practice after two days of heavy work would be best if skill development is emphasized. An athlete can maintain his level of fitness with three demanding workouts a week. Remember, the body needs rest to rebuild and repair damaged body tissue. Plan accordingly. Do not panic. Do not rush the conditioning process. Panic and rushing the process puts additional stress on the body which in turn leads to injuries. Proper planning will meet your objectives.

Year-Round Training

Athletes must train year-round. The short pre-season and regular season programs are not enough. Youth players may not be able to train year-round, but they can be active in other sports and programs. The off-season is the time to work on weaknesses and a strength development program. The year-round training programs used by many athletes today is one of the reasons for the longevity of the modern athlete. The athlete that goes from a lazy off-season to a demanding playing season and back to a lazy off season is creating a tremendous strain on his body, the heart in particular. This fluctuation of on-again and off-again conditioning takes its toll later on.

Strong conditioning can overcome many weakness in talent. A team's skill level decreases with an increase in fatigue. The less fatigue a team experiences during a game, the less skill, thinking and efficiency is lost. Hockey is among the most physically demanding sports. A well conditioned team can keep attacking an opponent.

Fatigue and Thinking

It is a well known fact that fatigue interferes with the thought process. The more fatigued the athlete, the slower his muscular response and ability to make decisions. Tired athletes may not only be slow in making decisions, but they will also often make poor decisions.

The first sign of a tired player on the ice is not a lack of power in his legs, but in his mind. Poor passes, wrong positioning, etc., are all indications of poor thinking and the first sign of fatigue. A breakdown in this area shows a poorly conditioned team.

Warming Up and Stretching

Stretching should not be done without a good warm-up. A problem with stretching exercises is that athletes do them as a means of warming up. Stretching is no longer recommended as a warmup. Stretching the cold muscles often contributes to pulled or torn muscles. Under the intense stress of competition, these injuries can eventually become serious. Warm up and then stretch. Many track and field coaches now do stretching exercises in the middle of their workouts when the body is heated up. Some athletes do stretching exercises in hot showers after practice. Some do not even do stretching exercises.

A good warm-up is to simply skate around the ice slowly and gradually increase speed to work up a good sweat. Get the body warm, and then begin the stretching exercises.

Water

Athletes must drink water to meet their body requirements. Many experts even recommend extra water before competition and before thirst develops. Water is mandatory for performance as performance deteriorates in the later stages of the game if the body lacks water.

Commercial drinks, soda and sugar drinks are not recommended. The body has trouble absorbing them and coverting them to energy. Water is best for fast body absorption.

Heat

As heat increases, sweat increases and so does the need for water. Hot arenas contribute to this problem. Dry land conditioning may be more of a problem if the area is hot and humid. Heat makes an athlete sweat more, and the humidity prevents sweat from evaporating which hinders the body's cooling process. If exercising outdoors, be careful. A hat is often a good protective measure from the sun's rays. Do not wear rubber or plastic material to cause the body to sweat and lose weight. This technique does not cause weight loss of body mass. It merely means a loss of water weight. This weight loss will soon be regained when the athlete drinks water or any liquid, or eats. Wearing a plastic or rubber suit creates a real danger of dehydration, which can be extremely dangerous.

Nausea, dizziness or disorientation are all signs of dehydration. If suspected, cool the body quickly.

Dry Land Programs

Many teams are using dry land conditioning in the off- and preseasons. Such a program is valuable, not only in physical conditioning, but also in mental aspects of preparing for the season. A good dry land program should not only contain running, but various running aspects. The following are examples of various exercises.

Fast Breaks: Fast breaks should be practiced from a dead stop, from a slow run and from half-speed runs. The athlete should alternate starting legs so the athlete does not become dependent on always starting with the same leg. It is amazing to observe how many hockey players have a preference on a certain leg for starts. If they are in a situation where they must start with their weak starting leg, their start is weak because the leg does a weak push in order to get the strong starting leg in position. Develop both legs equally so that an efficient start can be made with either leg.

Hopping: The hockey player should practice hopping with each leg and with both legs together. Hopping is good for increasing the work load of the legs and for increasing agility.

Backward Running: Backward running is excellent for extra work for the leg muscles. Backward running is also beneficial for agility.

Sideway Running: Excellent for agility development.

Jogging: Various speeds for different results. Excellent for warm-ups and cool-downs. Also, good for recovery between exercises like fast breaks, hopping, backward running, etc.

Many coaches have found road hockey to be an excellent means of getting in extra practice when ice time is hard to schedule, or even too expensive for adequate ice time. Some preseason programs use road hockey to prepare for the season before the ice in the rinks. Tennis courts make good dry land practice rinks, largely because they are enclosed which helps keep the ball in play. Many coaches have found strategy is easily taught within the road hockey environment. The players learn how to move and position themselves in relation to their teammates and the opposition. Some coaches, who do not have a hard surface area to practice on, have simply used a field with a tennis ball for a puck.

GAMES AND SPORTS

Various team and individual sports are excellent means of conditioning an athlete. They are fun and exciting. Simply drilling can become boring, and many of the players will perform the drills as a routine practice. Games will create a competitive atmosphere, with the players giving an all out effort. Motivation for the games is usually high. The games should be played at a fast pace. If necessary, change the rules to keep the game moving.

Team Sports: Basketball, field hockey, soccer, speedball, team handball and volleyball.

Individual Sports: Badminton, bicycling, karate, racquetball, handball, swimming, table tennis and tennis.

Nutrition

An athlete needs a well-balanced diet. There isn't much the coach can do about the kid's diet. In some ways the coach can pass on the following information in a effort to encourage his players to eat properly. The pre-game meal is not sufficient to counter a bad diet or poor eating habits. The coach must educate his players on nutrition and then hope for the best.

CARBOHYDRATES, FATS AND PROTEINS

The three nutrients the body requires are carbohydrates, fats and proteins. These nutrients provide the calories required for the energy, growth, repair and regulation of body processes. Carbohydrates and fats are the body's main sources of energy. Proteins are the body's main source of tissue repair. For the body to maintain efficiency, the athlete's diet should consist of 60-70 percent carbohydrates, 20-30 percent fats and 10-15 percent protein.

VEGETABLES AND FRUITS

Perhaps the biggest advance in dieting is the proof of the nutritional value of vegetables and fruits. Some say a proper diet also reduces the chances of cancer. Vegetables and fruits are excellent sources of carbohydrates and a source of energy. They are also low in fats. Salads are recommended with most meals, and in some cases they make an excellent meal by themselves. Be careful with salad dressings and mayonnaise. Be sure your choice isn't high in fat, sodium and sugar.

MEATS

Red meats are high in calories and provide more proteins than necessary. Ironically, the lower priced meats have less fat than the higher priced meats. The higher priced meats are more tender because the fat is thoroughly mixed throughout the meat fibers. Chicken and fish are a better source of meat proteins because they are leaner than beef. If the chicken and fish are batter fried then the calories rise considerably.

DESSERTS

Sugary desserts provide the body with many empty calories. Occasional desserts are not harmful if the diet is otherwise well balanced. Deserts can be a problem if they replace nutritional food.

VITAMINS AND MINERALS

Vitamins and minerals do not provide energy to the body. They help the body function properly and maintain good health. It is the maintenance of health and body efficiency that gives the body energy. A good diet will provide the body with adequate vitamins and minerals, and eliminate the need for supplements.

FIBER AND WATER

Fiber and water are essential to the diet. Adequate vegetables, fruits and cereals will provide sufficient fiber to the diet. Water is our most essential nutrient. Water is important to prevent dehydration, not only from exercise but also for daily living. The body needs about six glasses of water a day, and more when exercising. The body needs the water for most biochemical reactions. Tea, coffee and alcohol are diuretics, and tend to dehydrate the body. Athlete's who consume these drinks should increase their water intake. Many nutrition experts believe most people suffer from minor dehydration through the lack of sufficient water.

SODIUM AND SALT

Eliminate foods high in salt and sodium. Salt and sodium put an extra strain on the body, especially the heart. Athletes, in fact all people, do not need this additional work load on the body.

SIMPLE GUIDELINES

Eat a variety of foods.

Eat plenty of vegetables, fruits and grain products.

Maintain a diet low in fat, saturated fat and cholesterol.

Sugar, salt and sodium should be minimal.

Maintain proper body weight.

Pre- and Post-Game Meals

The pre-game meal is not as important as a proper daily diet. One meal before a game will not solve the daily problems surrounding a lack of nutrients. The pre-game meal should be comfortable to the athlete. Fatty foods and fried foods should be eliminated, while condiments, sauces and salts should be kept to a minimum. Easily digestible foods are best. The meal should be high in carbohydrates.

The post-game meal should also be high in carbohydrates, with meat for proteins to repair tissue, although a proper daily diet should not leave the athlete in demand for proteins after a game.

IX. Psychology of Coaching

Philosophy and Objectives

If you are going to be a coach, the first thing you must do is establish your coaching philosophy. Your philosophy is your beliefs, perceptions and principles for coaching. It may even be a good idea to write out your philosophies. Once you have a clear understanding of your philosophy, develop goals and objectives to enforce your philosophy. For example, are you coaching to win, to develop players, to have fun, or a combination of these factors. Each requires a different approach. Establish a philosophy so you know where you are going and how you are going to get there. To help in accessing your philosophies, ask yourself, "why are you coaching?"

A coach must have a philosophy for life and a philosophy for coaching. The two are very compatible. A philosophy is needed to give consistent direction to the coach and the players. Weak coaches have inconsistent philosophies or no philosophy. As a result, their teams lack direction. Lack of direction shows as pressure increases. Players in this situation have no criteria to guide them in their behavior, on and off the ice. Players know exactly were they stand when under the guidance of a strong philosophy. A consistent philosophy helps to firmly establish and remove the uncertainty of training rules, playing strategy, discipline, conduct, and goals.

Decision Making

Coaching involves making decisions. Good coaches make correct decisions, or at least better decisions. Your philosophy and objectives will help you make decisions as the situation presents itself. Your decisions will also have consistency as you follow the guidelines of your philosophy and objectives. This process is not only helpful to you as the coach, but it is extremely beneficial to the players because they will know exactly where you stand on issues, morals, attitudes, and ethics.

Good coaches make good decisions despite the circumstances. The coach will be hampered or facilitated in his decision making by the following factors:

1. TIME. Many times decisions must be made immediately. Procrastination will not be beneficial. When coaches are afraid to make a decision, the players recognize this hesitancy and lose faith in their leadership. Not making a firm decision can also split the group because each individual may see the answer differently. This can soon lead to a lack of unity as each player or clique is off on their own. Confident decisions can prevent the team from drawing their own conclusions as to how the coach should act.

2. INFORMATION. Decisions must be made with all the possible information available in the time frame. Coaches know this time frame may consist of a few seconds or days. If the decision can be delayed, delay the decision until such time as you have gathered more facts. Do not delay the decision for fear of making it or hoping the problem will solve itself in a few days. Only delay to gather more information.

3. ACCEPTANCE. Acceptance of a decision is best if the group supports the decision. This is not always possible. The players must realize this and sometimes accept the decision for the benefit of the group. Too often players accept decisions on the basis of how it affects them personally, not how it will benefit the team. Team unity and cohesion helps in the acceptance of decisions.

4. COACH'S POWER. The power of the coach is often a factor in the acceptance of decisions. Winning teams will tolerate more from the coach because the coach has more power and influence. Even though the players may not like the decisions, they will accept the them because they feel they are winning because of such decisions. Coaches that are losing often have difficulty keeping players on course because the players believe the losing is a result of the coach's decisions.

Coaching Style

Your coaching style will be a part of your philosophy. Coaching philosophies range from autocratic to democratic. The autocratic coach is demanding, authoritative and the ultimate decision maker. Players are his robots or puppets and they have no say in team decisions. The democratic coach makes no decisions, and the players have complete control. Good coaches, especially in youth programs, do not fall under either end of the scale. Very often the situation will dictate the style a coach selects. At times be autocratic, democratic at others, and sometimes in between. Learn the style for the situation.

Communications

Coaching is communications. The coach is always communicating with the team, management and fans. In many cases, even with the parents. Messages, directives, orders, demands, encouragement, praise, etc., must be given in a clear and precise manner. There must be no misunderstandings. Knowing when to praise, encourage, and reprimand is important. Timing is also important, as is the intensity of the message. There is a time to be mad, and a time to be calm, and time for various stages in between. Good, effective communicators know when and how.

Coaches must communicate. No communication leads to no interaction between the coach and players. Good communication helps motivation, interest, commitment and desire. Good communication also helps in receiving feedback from the players. Coaches need feedback. A coach cannot assume how his players feel or what they are thinking. The coach must know the thinking and feelings of his players. This knowledge is gained through feedback. Talk to the kids. Work with them. Laugh and have fun with them. Learn how to listen. Many coaches talk so much they fail to listen and observe. Listening and observing is how good coaches become good coaches.

Most communications are a result of body language, not by word of mouth. A coach's best assets are his eyes and ears. Learn to use them. Listen to what the players have to say. Watch for players' reactions. Watch their bodies for signs of dejection, elation, skepticism, etc. Body language is revealed through posture, gestures, facial expressions, mannerisms, etc. Very often the coach does not have to say anything, his body will express it for him. In verbal communication, the way you say it can be more effective than what you say. Things like the pitch and resonance of the voice is critical. The enunciation, speed and rhythm of your speech is also revealing. Of course, the loudness of the voice conveys a message.

The value of communications in coaching in invaluable. The players and coach must communicate freely and easily at all times. Communications going both ways must be understood exactly by each other so that no misinterpretation is possible. Misinterpreted messages can lead to needless disaster. The following are some guidelines that may be helpful.

1. Keep your messages or instructions as brief as possible.

2. Communicate clearly and precisely.

3. Do not jump to conclusions, know your facts.

4. Follow through on your instructions, messages and orders.

5. Use care in how you state your message.

Leadership

Coaches are leaders. Leaders get people to follow and achieve new and higher goals. Leadership assists the followers in developing their potential. This is the essence of coaching.

The team must have leadership. Everyone plays their role effectively on good teams. The coach leads, the players follow. The captains lead in their style and their teammates follow. Some players are not captains but still lead with their unit. Some goaltenders are also effective leaders. Some players are also good leaders off the ice. Good leadership will also help in developing team spirit and team unity – a cohesion among the players, team and organization.

Winning/Performance

Some coaches become so concerned about winning that they lose perspective after a loss. Losses will happen, learn from them. Good coaches never tell their players that they must win the game. Their practice sessions and pregame talks do not emphasize winning. The emphasis on winning is just putting more pressure on the athlete.

Flexibility

Flexibility does not mean being willing to break. Good coaches are able to bend without losing face. They set up policy so they can bend if needed with no detrimental effects to the position as a leader. Every problem has extenuating circumstances. Good leaders are aware of this and even prepare for such circumstances.

Selfishness

Good coaches provide a service to the team. The good coach places the team's well-being above his own. Some coaches coach for their own glory. Selfish coaches stand on shaky ground. Coaches must give the glory and credit to the players. Coaches must be humble but confident. Coaches must provide the service of leadership to the team.

The coach must not believe he is above all others. Coaches with overdeveloped egos are contradictions in philosophy and beliefs as they preach team unity, working and sharing for the team as they selfishly use the team to build their own egos.

Coaches must not take the game as a personal confrontation. Coaches often feel the purpose of the game is to determine who is the best coach. Some coaches believe when the team wins, it is the coach's victory, but when the team loses it is the player's loss as the players did not do what the coach instructed. Winning and losing are results, not processes. Good coaching is a process, the process of development. Study, analyze and teach the process, and winning will come. Winning isn't everything, making the effort too win is.

Silence

The group's words and actions give the group identity. When the team is silent, what is being conveyed? Actions and words are easily readable, right or wrong, good or bad. Silence is the deadly force. It is extremely powerful. Silence conveys a message. Learn to read silence.

Time to Reflect

Coaches must provide the players with time to reflect, and time to digest their learning and performances. Too often, coaches keep pushing the knowledge and performance to the point of weakness. Too much in too little time. When players have time to reflect they have time to get organized both physically and mentally.

The coach must not only give the players time to reflect and digest, but also give himself time to reflect and digest the coaching process. The coach must analyze his data from all perspectives.

The Facts

Remember, it is not enough to have the facts. The facts must be interpreted correctly. Too often coaches, rushing to solutions simply misinterpret or do not read the facts correctly.

Overkill

The coach who understands team dynamics will use as little force as possible to get the job done. By using as little force as needed, the coach is able to save the use of increased force for more important and vital situations. Do not use overkill. Save it.

Force

There will come times when the coach must act with force. Good leaders know when the right time requires action. Experience will teach timing. Even though the strong force is needed, remember that the use of such force could injure someone. The repercussions may not show itself immediately, but may reveal itself later in the season or even in future years. Players do not forget how they are treated. It is important to remember that when force is used, do not to make it a personal attack.

Keep It Simple

Look for simple solutions first. Often the solution is right in front of our eyes and we fail to see it. We look in all directions, analyze, and look to complex solutions. We become swept up by the excitement and drama of the moment. Our emotions can influence our decisions and the decision making process.

The Obvious

Many times the solutions to problems seem obvious. But the obvious is often a deception. The obvious is often a cover to the real problem. Learn to peek under the obvious.

Sometimes players will come to the coach to discuss a problem and ask questions on the subject, but not directly related to the problem. This technique is known as the "feeling out" process. The player is feeling out the coach to get up the nerve to ask the desired question, or to see if the coach is receptive toward the player and his problem. Very often these player problems may not seem serious to the coach, but to the player these problems are very serious. Many times these problems are not related to hockey, but are personal.

Power

A wise leader must never be self-centered. The leader must provide service to the team, players, and management. This is were power of the coach lies. The coach that gives the wise leadership through his service to the team receives power. Power is not taken from the players, nor is it granted by the position. Power is earned from the players through cooperation, mutual respect and sharing. Power that is demanded without being earned or through the position, is shaky and weak. Shaky and weak power does not hold up when the pressure is on.

Leaders must never abuse their power. They must never demand more than is required to meet the goal. Overkill is not always necessary. Handle power with respect. Abuse of power will lead to rebellion within the team.

Awareness

The coach must not only be aware of what is happening to the group, but also of himself. This understanding will help the coach decide on action or silence, intervention or withdrawal. The aware coach is able to facilitate the team process and help move it in the right direction.

Recognition

The coach should not look for credit for everything he accomplishes. He should not strive for recognition. Good coaches get the job done by facilitating the players effort. Good coaches stand in the background while the players share the glory. Good coaches know their role, and enjoy helping the group. Players appreciate a coach who lets them share the honors. Players do not like coaches who are selfish and promote themselves.

Know-It-All

Many coaches assume they are hired because they know everything. Unfortunately, this belief is easily noticed by the players. No one has all the answers. When the time comes, the coach may have to admit, "I do not know." Wise coaches are not afraid to listen to their players and accept their advice if it is valuable to the team.

Tenacity

Good coaches work through discouragement, apathy, rejection, disappointment and other problems. Weak coaches function well when everything is going their way. Weak coaches do not hold up to adversity. Good coaches persist in leadership and follow through with commitments. They do not "jump ship" on the team. They experience joy, laughter, sadness with the players.

Accountability

Whether coaches like it or not, they must be held accountable for their actions. This is accepted and should be understood when the job is taken. No coach or leader is beyond approach.

Loyalty

Leaders must have loyalty to the team, management, school or city they represent. Lack of loyalty shows a lack of respect and a selfish attitude. A coach may have to dismiss captains or other players who lack loyalty if all efforts to help the player fail. Management should dismiss a coach for lack of loyalty because it can spread throughout the team.

Disagreements do not necessarily mean a lack of loyalty exists. Disagreements can present alternative solutions to problems. Disagreements can lead to compromises and a possible better solution. Wise leaders know the difference between disagreements and a lack of loyalty. Wise coaches never let disagreements divide the team.

Responsibility

The coach must take his position seriously and be responsible. Being a coach is a privilege, not a right. The coach must never carry out his duties at the expense of his players. The coach works for the players.

Leaders are responsible for their own actions. What they say they must do. They cannot say one thing and do another. Such action is interpreted by the players as deception and the coach is perceived as devious.

Weak coaches avoid responsibility, great coaches accept it.

Respect

Coaches should be courtious and respectful to their subordinate leaders and players. Coaches who cannot respect others cannot earn it.

Pompous Behaviour

Pompous behavior and appearance will promote contempt among the players. Usually, this attitude is readily noticeable in the dress and mannerisms of the coach. A pompous coach uses the players as a means to his glory, and tools for the coach's personal success. In these situations, players feel used and they will resent it.

Assistant Coaches

If you hire an assistant coach, he must have the ability to carry out assigned duties. The coach must trust his subordinates and help in their development to be future coaches and leaders. Assistant coaches, when carrying out a delegated responsibility, must be held accountable for their actions and results.

Weak coaches surround themselves with weak assistants. Weak assistants have problems carrying out responsibilities.Good coaches hire good assistants. Good leadership means good teams.

The Opposition

Simply stated: Never underestimate the opposition and never over estimate your own abilities as a coach.

Decisiveness

Good coaches are decisive. They make decisions and make them at the correct time. Indecisive coaches are doomed to failure. Delays in the decision making process often lead to a lack of uncertainty. This is readily noticeable by the players who, in turn, develop a lack of confidence in their coach's ability to lead.

Rewards

Never reward a player or assistant for doing less than expected. This lessens the reward and makes it less valuable. Rewards must be earned. The coach's main concern is the rewarding of his team and not himself. Small rewards, such as gratitude, concern, interest, help, etc., are often the greatest rewards a coach can make to his players. The return benefits will multiply with loyalty and other honorable traits.

Defeats

Loses are part of coaching, and should be expected, but not necessarily accepted. It is OK to grieve after a loss, but make it short. One game does not a season make. Always remember, there is work to be done. Learn from a loss. Defeat can be a great teacher if used to enhance the future. Remember, leaders determine the future. Do not let a temporary defeat slow, stop or destroy you.

Motivation

Is motivation the coach's responsibility? To some extent it may be but it is also the player's responsibility to motivate himself. If the athlete is not motivated to play and practice, then maybe he should not be playing the game. Good coaching will help the players maintain their high level of motivation. Weak and poor coaches can stifle and destroy an athlete's motivation. Motivation is often directly related to the quality of the coaching. Coaching may not improve motivation but weak coaching can hinder it.

Control

Some coaches feel that letting the players take responsibility is a loss of their ability to control the players. Letting the players take responsibility is not giving them free rein to do as they please. Structure is still prevalent and is needed more when control is eased. Players must be guided within the structure. This type of coaching takes extra work and trust in your players.

Humor

The leader must have a sense of humor. Humor is appreciated by the players and can lead to good rapport between the coach and players. Humor must be used carefully, it is a double edged sword. Humor at the wrong time or interpreted the wrong way can lead to disaster. Coaches should not use humor just for the sake of using it. There is nothing worse then someone trying to be funny.

Anger

At the right time and when necessary, anger is justified. Anger can be accepted by the players and forgotten with no hard feelings, but, sarcasm and contempt is taken personally and is not forgotten.

A coach who does not employ anger when the players are expecting it and feel they deserve it, may carry the message to the players that the coach does not care. This may not be true, however. The coach is not judged by what he does, but rather by what they think he does.

Rules

Do not have a rule you cannot enforce. If there is something that you want the players to do but you cannot enforce it then it may be best to make it an expectation. A list of team rules should be as brief as possible. Each rule should be relevant and fair. There can be no exceptions to the rules because all players should benefit or suffer equally. The players should know the penalty for breaking a rule.

Rules are negative statements, and the establishment of rules seems to convey the idea that the players are not able to stay within the expected behavior of the team. When a rule is made it is almost like saying that the player is not capable of expected behavior and must be forced to stay in line.

The use of rules varies from coach to coach and with different levels and ages of the players. The coach and the team should decide on the rules needed to meet the philosophy of the coach, team and players.

Great and Weak Coaches

Weak coaches tell their players what to do. Great coaches build habits and change behavior so that the players know how and are able to do what is needed. Building habits and changing behavior is accomplished through practice sessions with good teaching.

X. Youth Coaching Tips

Coaching in the youth program is a very difficult job, and requires excellent teachers. Remember, coaching youngsters is not a watered down version of coaching older players. Young players' needs, desires and abilities are different than older players. Good youth program coaches are able to reach and understand the kids and teach to their level. Good coaches reach the spirit of the kids and help them develop toward their goals. Weak coaches simply give drills and lectures and hope it all falls into place. When that does not happen, they blame the kids and their lack of ability or motivation. An honest assessment may show that the problem is not the kids, but a coaching or teaching problem.

When a coach takes over a youth team, he must access the ability, interests and motivation of the players so he can devise his coaching plan. The drills, strategy and expectations must be in line with the ability of the players. A good coach knows what the progression of skill teaching is so that the kids can learn their hockey skills to their best ability. By accessing the players' ability, the coach knows where he must start the player's skill learning. If the team is very unskilled then the drills and philosophy for the team must develop from the beginning stages. If the players are more advanced, then the coach can start the development at the middle stages of the skill progression scale. Strategy will also depend on the ability of the players. Does the team need the basic strategy, the advanced level strategy or a strategy somewhere in between?

Four Stages of Development

There are four basic stages of development:

1. Lack of Ability – This usually applies to the youngest age group, but it can also apply to the later age group if the players are novices. Skill learning for the players at this level starts at the beginning of the skill progression stage. This is an important stage because it lays the foundation for future ability. If the skills are learned correctly at this stage, then good players develop.

2. Progress Stage – This is the stage when you see rapid development by the players. Concentration is improving. Things may still look awkward but development is becoming evident.

3. Pre-proficiency Level – The awkward stage is almost gone. The skills and moves of the players are smoothing out, more refined and automatic. A lack of strength prevent some skills from being fully realized. Strategy and an understanding of the game, or skill is becoming stronger. The cognitive abilities are getting better. At this level, the gap between the good and poor players is widening.

4. Proficiency Level – The skills are highly refined at this level. The moves are smooth and refined. There are very few players at this level. Some teams in the older age youth programs may not have any players at this level.

On Task

A coach must know these four levels to access his team's ability. From this ability assessment the coach is able to devise his drills, strategy and philosophy for his team. The less skilled the performer, the more simple the teaching. Simple teaching does not mean less effective teaching, it means less complex teaching; more demonstrations and less talking; more on task practice and less complicated instruction. On task means physically practicing the skill. Actually shooting a puck is on task, listening to the coach explain how to shoot a puck is not on task. Naturally, kids needs all the on task time the coach can provide. Talking should be quick, simple and directed to the key points.

Dead Time

Eliminate dead time. Do not let the practice session have the players standing around waiting to do something. Keep the players on task as much as possible. Plan drills so that the waiting line is short. If possible, use each end of the rink and the middle for the same drill. This gives smaller groups more on task time. If you use relay drills, have as few players as possible in line waiting their turn. Use more relay lines. Players standing in line, waiting their turn, become bored and restless. Sometimes this waiting situation can become a discipline problem.

Discipline

Keep players active and moving. This will help eliminate problems. Eliminate dead time. If the coach must take disciplinary action, it should be short and quick, with as little disruption as possible. Sometimes just a stern look can solve the problem. Sometimes just ignoring the problem is enough, while on other occassions a gesture, like pointing a finger or shaking a fist, is sufficient. If stronger measures are needed, the reprimand must be clear, firm, at the proper time, directed at the correct target and never be a personal attack. Discipline must be fair and certain players must not be continually singled out.

Coaches must be aware that what he sees as a problem may not be a problem from a player's perspective. Sometimes the situation may just be a little fun time, nothing serious, just a break in the tension. A little fun or laughter may not hurt the practice or learning environment. A coach should not intervene unless it is really necessary.

Readiness

When accessing the ability of the team, the coach must be aware of the readiness principle. The readiness principle pertains to the players being prepared or ready for the mental and physical demands of the skill. Learning cannot take place if the coach is teaching a technique that the players do not have the physical strength or skill level to execute. Knowing progressive levels of learning will help the coach decide where the most effective starting point is for skill development. Advanced strategy is of little use to players if they do not understand game patterns and basic strategies. Mentally the player is not ready for the advanced level.

Foundations

Youth coaches build foundations, solid foundations. The various hockey skills are learned from the beginning. If necessary, the coach may have to backtrack for the players to understand the skill foundations. Fundamentals are the foundations to strategy. Poor passing, skating, goaltending and puck control lead to poor strategy. Coaches must lay a strong and solid foundation in skill learning so the players develop properly.

Interest

Good coaching and teaching lead to strong interest and motivation by the players. If the drills and strategy are geared to the level of the players, then the game is more fun. The readiness principle is a strong factor in maintaining interest. Kids want to learn. As the player's readiness develops, the coach must challenge the kids with new and advanced techniques. Progress from simple to advanced, not too fast and not too slow.

Challenging the kids is difficult when there is a large variance in abilities among the players. Some players may even be in the proficiency stage, while others may be in the lack of ability stage. Coping with the different abilities is what coaching is all about.

Remember, youth coaches develop players, and you do not develop players by telling the weaker players to sacrifice playing and practice time in favor of better players. It is the coach's job to make sure everyone has an equal opportunity to develop.

Team Personality

Every team has its own personality. The coach must recognize this. The same personnel from year-to-year can still take on a different personality each year, much the same way a player's personality changes as he grows. The coach can have some effect on the teams personality but it is limited. The coach must adjust with the team, within reason.

Creativity

Youth coaches should be creative, which means being willing to experiment, to try new things. Creativity can bring variety and fun to practices.

Teacher

Youth coaches are teachers. They teach skills and strategy. They teach on-ice and off-ice skills. Coaches have a feel for the job. Coaches are teachers and not text books. Books are good and helpful, but they are only tools. The words have to be interpreted and executed by the coach, while fitting the team's personality and philosophy.

Learning Environment

Youth coaches must establish a learning environment right away. Aspects such as skills, strategy and understanding of the game must be developed as well as the ancillary aspects of the game. Safety factors or rules, like no throwing snow, tape or paper should be allowed in the dressing room. Clean dressing rooms, punctuality, stopping when the coach is talking, etc., are all rules or expectations that the kids learn for life.

Talk On Their Level

Youth coaches have to talk to their players in a language the kids understand. Expressions like "angle", or "slot" may not be fully understood by some players. Never ask the players if they understand, because most players will say yes even though they may not have a clear and precise understanding. Out of fear of embarrassment, many players will not admit to not understanding. In some cases, the coach will have to ask some players to explain their answer. Never assume the players know this or that – find out for sure.

"Hummmms" and "Ahhhhs"

When talking to players, or giving a talk to parents, do not express the "hummmms" and "ahhhhs." If the coach is lost in thought it is best to say nothing and just have silence. Talk naturally. Do not cloud the conversation by constantly searching for the right or impressive words. Say what you have to say. Do not drive your players nuts with "hummmms" and "ahhhhs".

When talking, do not oscillate, bounce from one foot to the other foot, or move around. Be stationary. Movement is distracting. Stand strong and solid to help create the image of authority, confidence and knowledge. Also, when talking to the players on the ice, bring them close. Do not yell instructions across the rink. The echo in some rinks garbles shouted words.

Look at 'em

Coaches must look at their players when talking to them. A coach who lets his eyes wander shows a lack of sincerity or interest to the players. When the coach tells a player something, he must make eye contact to show authority and validity in what is being said.

Look Energetic

Coaches should look energetic when coaching. If a coach is leaning on the boards for practice, or moving around the ice in a slow and lazy manner, he may be showing a lack of interest to the players. This may not necessarily be the case, but it may be interpreted that way. Coaches should talk to the players as if he is enjoying the experience. The coach's body language should show interest and vitality. The dress of the coach often shows interest in the activity. A coach that takes off his business suit and puts on a sweat suit shows that he is getting ready for action.

XI. Offense/Defense Tactics

Scoring goals is one of the main purposes of the game. Every player should practice this skill.

SHOOTING IN STRIDE

Hockey players should develop the skill of shooting in stride. Shooting in stride entails the skill of shooting the puck while continuing to skate. A shooter cannot afford to coast, position his feet, lift a leg, or take an extra stickhandle in order to get the puck away. Such delays work in the goaltender's favor. A goaltender who recognizes such faults, knows the player is getting ready to shoot and consequently has more time to react. A shooter guilty of delay faults will find he has lost an excellent scoring opportunity.

To shoot in stride, the player must learn to shoot off either foot and with his feet in virtually any position. A player who becomes proficient in this skill will score many goals. Since a shot taken in stride gives no forewarning, the goaltender has less time to read and react to the shot. It is often the element of surprise that will beat the goaltender. It is extremely difficult to beat a good goaltender when he is ready for the shot.

TAKING THE PASS AND SHOOTING

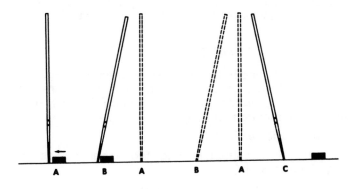

Diagram 11-1

The skill of taking a pass and shooting quickly must be highly developed through practice. The skills for pass receiving and shooting are coordinated into one smooth motion. In diagram 11-1, the player receives the pass at position 'A'. The player gives the puck a good cushion by letting the stick ride back with the pass to position 'B'. With this cushion, the stick is moving back into position for the sweeping action of the shot. At the end of the cushion, the shooter moves into the shot be sweeping the stick forward to position 'C,' with the shooting mechanics discussed under puck control in the shooting section.

A player should be able to take a pass and shoot quickly with a forehand and backhand shot. Many goals have been scored by the player taking the pass and getting the shot away before the goalie has time to react. Conversely, many scoring opportunities have been squandered because a player was not able to get the shot away quickly. In fact, more goals have been missed than scored.

THE FAKE SHOT

The fake shot is perhaps one of the easiest and most effective methods of deceiving the goaltender. The simplest method is to drop the shoulder, usually the right shoulder for a right-handed shot, and make a shooting motion without letting the puck leave the stick. Do not make the fake too elaborate or complicated. Too much action in performing the fake will not fool the goaltender. Goaltenders seem to senses whether or not an opponent plans to shoot or not.

There are numerous types of fake shots. Any type of shot can be faked. The slap, the sweep, the flip, and others can all be faked effectively with the forehand and backhand. The fake shot works well when deceiving an opponent in order to get closer to the goal. When approaching a defender, the attacker can use a fake to catch his opponent flat-footed so the attacker may gain a shooting advantage.

SKATING AND BODY FAKES

Various skating and body fakes can be used to deceive the goaltender. Deception is used to make the goaltender commit himself so that the shooter can gain an advantage during a scoring attempt. Some skating and body fakes include:

1. Lifting one leg as if to shoot.

2. Coasting as if to shoot, making stride for an increase in speed and then shooting.

3. Shifting the weight to the front foot as if to shoot.

4. Using a shooting arm movement, but not losing control of the puck.

5. Performing the shot mechanics, but letting the blade of the stick ride over the puck so the puck does not travel to the goal but remains with the shooter.

There are many fakes the player can invent. The key to a successful fake is in keeping the motion subtle or sly. Keep it simple and do not over act the fake.

THE GOAL SCORING AREA

Goals have been scored from almost anywhere near the goal net. Even shots from behind the net have deflected into the goal. Because the puck can take unusual bounces, many coaches stress shooting at all times. The more shots a team takes, the better the odds that one will go in for a goal. To a certain extent this may be true, however, some areas are more advantageous for scoring than others. Attackers should strive to work the puck into these more advantageous areas.

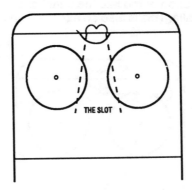

Diagram 11-2

Diagram 11-2 shows the most advantageous area for goal scoring. This area is called the slot. Offensive strategy nearly always calls for a player to work his way into this area if the team hopes to score.

BEATING THE GOALTENDER

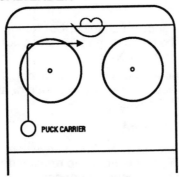

Diagram 11-3

One of the best ways to beat a goaltender is to approach the goal net from the side and cut across the front of the goal net as illustrated in diagram 11-3. This attack action forces the goaltender to stay in the net and keeps him from leaving the crease and reducing the shooting angle. With the attacker approaching from the side, the goaltender is forced to move to the far post. If the goaltender moves too soon or too late the attacker can shoot or slip the puck past the goalie. This is also an excellent time for the attacker to use a fake.

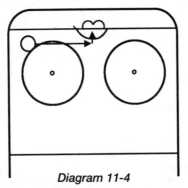

Diagram 11-4

Notice in diagram 11-4 that if the goaltender moves too soon the near post area is open for the shooter.

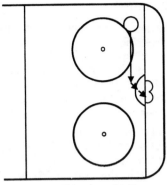
Diagram 11-5

In diagram 11-5 the goaltender moves too late and the shooter has the far post area open for the shot.

ACCURACY VERSUS POWER WHEN SHOOTING

Accurate shots tend to beat a goaltender because they are placed in the most difficult spots for the goaltender to defend. Hard shots will beat a goaltender because he is not able to react quickly enough to stop the shot. Both have advantages and disadvantages. A slow, accurate shot gives the goaltender extra time to react to the puck, while the hard, inaccurate shot may be useless because it is not in the correct place. Overall, a combination of power and accuracy is best and should be the aim of both coach and player when shooting.

THE SHOT VERSUS THE DEKE

Circumstances determine which is more important. If the goalie is well out of the net and the shooter has no scoring angle, then the deke is more advantageous. If the goaltender is deep in the net, then the shot may be the better choice. Scorers develop an instinct as to which is the better choice for the situation. Experience and practice develops this instinct.

REBOUNDS

The shooter should always follow his shot in case there is an opportunity for a rebound. A teammate in the area should also be ready for the rebound. After making the initial stop, the goaltender is often unprepared or out of position for a second shot. The rebound shot should be made quickly. The quick rebound shot often happens too quickly for the goaltender to stop.

SCREEN SHOTS AND TIP-INS

Screening the goaltender is the skill of using the body to block the vision of the goaltender. By being in position to screen the goaltender from the puck, the player is also in position to play the rebound or deflect the shot on goal. Blocking the goaltender's view makes it extremely difficult for the goalie to position himself and play the puck correctly. Sometimes the goalie will put himself off balance or leaning the wrong way to see the puck.

The deflected shot or tip-in is very difficult to stop because of the sudden change of direction of the puck. Often the puck is deflected away from the goalie as he moves to stop the initial shot. Usually, the deflection is too close to the goaltender for him to readjust to the puck.

An attacker can also use a defender as a screen. Quite often a defenseman backing towards his goal will set an excellent screen. Some shots are even accidentally deflected off the goaltender's teammates. In most cases, the best screen shots are low or along the ice.

SCRAMBLES

In scrambles, the shot must be made quickly and with no hesitation. If the puck is on its edge or bouncing haphazardly, the shooter should shoot the puck with a stiff wrist (no wrist snap). Doing this will keep the puck low and powerful. Snapping the wrists when the puck is on edge will often cause the puck to flip over the stick blade.

ORIENTATION OF THE NET

During a game, an attacker should always know exactly where the goal net is, no matter what his position or whether he is even facing the goal net. Even with his back to the goal net, the player should be able to know where the net is located in relation to his position. Many times, especially during scrambles, an attacker will not have time to look for the goal net and its openings. In these situations, the attacker has a strong advantage if he is able to shoot, slap or push the puck to the goal net without taking time to locate the goal net. Very often this quickness will catch the goaltender unprepared. The markings on the ice, marks on the boards, etc., will help the attacker know were the goal net is. Remember, no matter how much the player moves, the goal net will always be in the same position.

IMPROVING THE SHOT OFF THE ICE

One must practice is if he hopes to improve his shot. Practice sessions must not be haphazard or careless. The player can practice his shot by using a shooting board and a back drop. This can be set up in a basement, driveway or any small area.

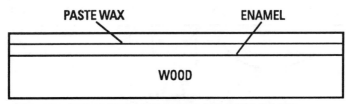

EDGE VIEW (ENLARGED) OF PRACTICE SHOOTING BOARD

Diagram 11-6

The smoother the shooting board (diagram 11-6), the closer the board will be to ice conditions. Almost any board or piece of plywood can be used. A heavier board will work best because it will be more stable. A smooth surface can be achieved by sanding and waxing. Paste wax works better than liquid wax, providing a smooth, slippery surface. If several coats of enamel, preferably a light color, are applied to the wood surface before waxing, the surface will be even smoother and harder. Harder surfaces will last longer because the board will be subjected to a lot of wear from the stick and puck sliding across the surface. The shooting board should be large enough for the shooter to be able to apply the proper shooting mechanics (2 feet x 1 1/2 feet is usually adequate). The backdrop can be almost anything that will stop a puck. A canvas backdrop works extremely well. A large old rug can also serve the purpose. The canvas and rugs will cushion the shot. A garage door or wall can also serve as a backstop, although the edges of the puck will chip from contact with the hard wall or door.

Rounding the Goal Net

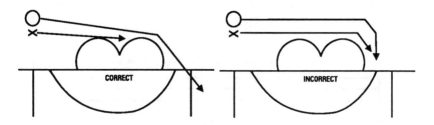

Diagram 11-7

Diagram 11-7 illustrates the correct way for a puck carrier to move around the goal net. He should hug the far post as he breaks to open ice. When he hugs the post, notice how the checker is forced to stop his chase or go into the goal net. When the puck carrier goes wide as in the incorrect diagram, the checker is able to cut the angle and catch the puck carrier.

Covering the Man

Covering or checking a man is often a difficult skill. Coaches do not spend enough time in developing this skill. The checker will have to stop, start, cut, turn and body check with split second timing. Like a mirror, the checker must imitate many of the actions of his check. A poor skater will have extreme difficulty in staying with his man. Some skaters, although they may be slow, have the agility to do the job. The assets of quickness and anticipation will help prevent the checker from winning the battle.

COVERING THE MAN WITHOUT THE PUCK

In covering an attacker who does not have the puck, the checker should always try to be between his man and the puck, and as close to his man as possible. The checker is not allowed to make any attempt to interfere with the player. A checker that covers his man well will also prevent the opposition from attempting to pass to his check. When a checker prevents a pass to his check, then he is doing an excellent job even though he may not touch the puck. Many a puck carrier is baffled or makes a bad play because he has no team-mate to pass to. Forcing the opposition into making bad plays is good defensive hockey. Gaining puck possession on plays like this puts the defensive team into the offensive attack.

COVERING THE MAN WITH THE PUCK

When covering the puck carrier, the defensive player should maintain a position between the puck carrier and the goal. This position means that the puck carrier has to go through the defender to reach the goal.

The checker must watch his man and the play at the same time. Rarely, should he turn his back on either, but, if forced to do so, he must immediately pick up both his man and the play.

If the attacker beats his checker, the checker must not slow down or coast. The checker is in position where he must speed up and catch his opponent by back-checking. Very often it is possible to catch the attacker as he will sometimes slow down to take a pass, shoot or deke. The attacker may even slow down thinking he has beaten his check and is home free.

STICK CHECKING

The hockey stick can be used to great advantage in checking. By letting go with the bottom hand and by manipulating the stick with the top hand, the checker is able to get considerable reach in deflecting the puck or stealing the puck from the puck carrier. The stronger the arms and upper body, the more powerful the execution.

In covering the man, there are three basic stick checks: the poke check, the hook check and the stick lift check. Each of these checks will have variations and styles will differ with each individual. In maneuvering for the stick checks, the checker should use a short skating stride for agility. The feet should be a little further apart with the skate blades well dug into the ice for a strong base. The digging in should be with the flat of the skate, not with the toe of the blade. The knees should be bent and springy for any required change of movement.

THE POKE CHECK

The poke check is simply poking the stick out at the puck. It is a jab or stab at the puck to knock the puck away from the carrier. Timing is the most important factor and it is learned through practice. It is a good idea to hold the stick back at the side of the body; then, as the puck carrier is approaching, the checker is able to give the stick a good thrust or poke forward. On completion of the poke check, the checker is often able to gain control of the puck as the puck carrier will often overskate the puck. The poke check can be use in checking from the side, from behind or from in front of the opponent. The poke check is one of the most valuable defensive tricks. Practice it and learn it.

Perhaps the biggest mistake in performing the poke check is to hold the stick too far out in front of the body. By holding the stick too far in front, the checker is unable to get a good thrust at the puck. The puck carrier will often use the end of the stick as a guide to time his deke, fake or just speed to get around his checker. By holding the end of the stick blade closer to the body, the puck carrier can often be led or brought in closer to the checker for a more effective poke at the puck.

THE HOOK CHECK

The hook check is a valuable trick because if it is executed properly it can give immediate possession of the puck to the checker. The angle at the stick blade and shaft of the hockey stick is used to catch or hook the puck. The timing and thrust are much like those used in the poke check, except the stick must be held low enough to the ice, almost flat, to prevent the puck from slipping underneath the stick. This skill is usually performed from the side or from behind the puck carrier. It can be performed from in front of the puck carrier but it is very difficult.

THE SWEEP CHECK

The sweep check is similar to the hook check, except that the stick is swept along the ice to hook the puck.

THE STICK LIFT CHECK

This check is usually performed when the checker is alongside the puck carrier. The checker puts his stick under the puck carrier's stick so he can lift the stick off the ice. With the checker's stick under and controlling the attackers stick, the checker is able to gain control of the puck.

BODY CHECK

A checker should not attempt a body check unless he is ready and positive that he will hit his opponent. To prepare himself, the checker must line up his opponent and give himself a solid base. For the solid base, the checker's feet are spread a little farther apart than normal and the knees are flexed. The body is balanced on the flat of the skate blade. The body lean is well forward and the buttocks are protruded back so that balance is maintained. The forward lean is at the hips, the back is relatively straight and the head is held well up.

Contact is made with the shoulder, hip or upper body. The checker must not just hit his opponent, but hit through him. The hitting through action is accomplished by pushing or driving hard with the legs immediately prior to and during contact. A principle of physics can be applied to body checking. The greater force is applied through the rate of acceleration upon contact, rather than through the speed upon contact.

The body check need not always be violent and vigorous. Sometimes, just getting the body in the way of an opponent is very effective. A good drill for practicing body checking is to have defensive players use hockey sticks with the blades cut off. A player having no blade on his stick will be unable to handle the puck and will be forced into playing the body.

THREE LINES OF DEFENSE

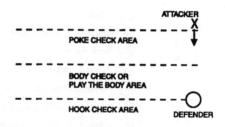

Diagram 11-8

Diagram 11-8 shows the three lines of defense that a defender can utilize. By using the poke check as a first attempt, the body check as a second attempt and the hook check as a third, the checker has set up three lines of defense against the puck carrier. If the poke check fails, the checker is still able to use the body check or hook check. A coach who stresses only the body check is having his players use only the one line of defense. In the event the checker misses on all three attempts, he must pursue the attacker.

XII. Strategy

Key to Diagrams

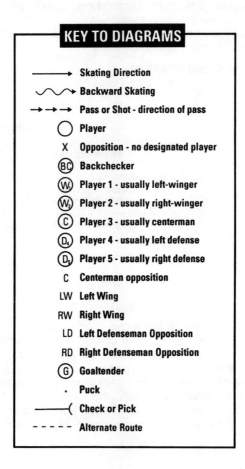

KEY TO DIAGRAMS

⟶ Skating Direction

〰⟶ Backward Skating

→ → → Pass or Shot - direction of pass

◯ Player

X Opposition - no designated player

Ⓑⓒ Backchecker

Ⓦ₁ Player 1 - usually left-winger

Ⓦ₂ Player 2 - usually right-winger

Ⓒ Player 3 - usually centerman

Ⓓ₄ Player 4 - usually left defense

Ⓓ₅ Player 5 - usually right defense

C Centerman opposition

LW Left Wing

RW Right Wing

LD Left Defenseman Opposition

RD Right Defenseman Opposition

Ⓖ Goaltender

. Puck

⟼(Check or Pick

- - - - - Alternate Route

Diagram 12-1

Introduction To Team Strategy

A coach, in devising his strategy, can adhere to one of the systems outlined, or he can take pieces from each system. He must, however, keep in mind that stages must flow smoothly into each other. For example, a fore-checking philosophy must flow smoothly into the back-checking strategy, without a scramble for new positions; a back-checking strategy must coordinate with the defensive strategy; a defensive strategy must coordinate with the breakout play; a breakout play must work into the attack; and the attack must develop into the fore-checking patterns.

Hockey is a fast moving game that switches from offense to defense in the blink of an eye. An attack is of little value if there is an immediate switch of puck possession and players are caught out of position for defensive play. It is imperative that strategy flows from one stage to the other. In fact, all strategy flows in a circular pattern as in diagram 12-2.

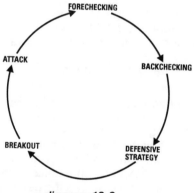

diagram 12-2

Basic Team Strategies

Hockey strategy breaks down into two basic situations: the one-on-one and the two-on-one. Offensive team strategy is usually geared toward developing a two-on-one situation, in order to gain advantage for puck possession or for a scoring opportunity. Defensive strategy is geared toward *preventing* a two-on-one situation by countering with at least a one-on-one stand against each offensive threat.

All situations are an extension of the one-on-one and the two-on-one situations. The three-on-two, three-on-one, two-on-two, etc., are simply multiples of the two-on-one and one-on-one.

When utilizing or countering these situations, a team should have a consistent philosophy of execution. If each player knows his responsibilities during a given situation, he will be able to react in an organized manner without confusing his duties.

Basic team strategies will be discussed, both defensively and offensively.

Basic Team Strategies – Defensive

Defensive strategy is based on playing the percentages. This means it is better to force an opponent to take a shot from further out, compared to in close. There is a greater percentage in stopping long shots than close ones. Playing the percentages also means forcing shots from an angle rather than the slot (central position in front of the goal net). Defensively, a team tries to keep the opposition from controlling the puck in the slot because of the high percentage of scoring possibilities in this area.

Playing the percentages is particularly evident where the opposition has the man advantage as in the two-on-one or three-on-two situations. This happens quite frequently when the opposition tries to gain a man advantage when on the attack. Since a defender cannot be in two places at once, the coverage must be geared toward the most dangerous man, or the man in better position to score.

In defensive situations, and even the offensive strategy, the goaltender must be involved. Too many times, the goaltender is simply left to play the shot, no matter where it comes from. If the goaltender knows what his teammates are doing, he can react quicker through anticipation. If the goaltender and the defensemen coordinate their efforts, they have an excellent chance of neutralizing the attack. If a back-checker enters the defensive strategy, he must also have definite responsibilities so everyone knows what is happening and what will happen.

Defensemen, in playing their attacker(s), should use an imaginary guideline as their back-up (diagram 12-3). This back-up line is just off the goal post and along the edge of the slot area. Later diagrams will show how these guidelines come into play.

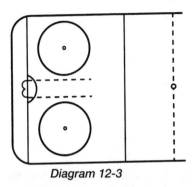

Diagram 12-3

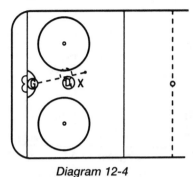

Diagram 12-4

ONE-ON-ONE – DEFENSIVE

The defenseman (diagram 12-4) must play the body and not the puck. His main purpose is to force the attacker to the side and out of the slot, or force the shot wide of the goal net. The defenseman must not lunge at his check or any similar action that would give the attacker clear access to the goal should he miss his check. This type of play may be possible if a back-checker is in good position to cover. A back-checker on the one-on-one plays the puck, unless the goalie clears it. The back-checker must be alert because the goalie may clear the puck to the back-checker for a quick break out of the end zone.

By playing the puck carrier's body, the defenseman leaves the goalie with a sight line (clear line of vision) to the puck. If the defenseman is playing the puck, he will often be positioned in front of the puck which will likely screen the puck from the goalie. In diagram 12-4, the defenseman is playing the body and leaves the goalie with a sight line to the puck. The dotted circle represents the defenseman when playing the puck. Notice how he is blocking the goalie's vision of the puck.

If the puck carrier is attacking down the center ice area (diagram 12-5), the defenseman must force him to the side and out of the slot area, so a possible shot by the attacker will be from a poor angle.

The defenseman must always play the man after the shot so the goalie or back-checker has time to clear or control the puck. The defenseman must not let the attacker slip past him for a second chance at scoring or regaining possession of the puck.

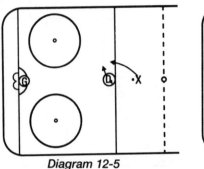

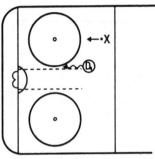

Diagram 12-5   Diagram 12-6

If the puck carrier approaches from the side (diagram 12-6), the defenseman should follow his imaginary guideline back to the goal to prevent his check from cutting into the slot. The defenseman simply keeps the attacker to the outside so his shot will be from a poor angle. If the defenseman moves to close to the boards and plays his attacker head-on, then it is easier for the attacker to cut into the slot for a quick shot. Another advantage to staying on the guideline is in case another attacker moves into the attack for a two-on-one situation.

If the attacker is alone and the defenseman has a strong possibility of stopping the attacker early by moving closer to the boards, then such a risk may be worthy. Remember, there must be a strong possibility.

TWO-ON-ONE – DEFENSIVE

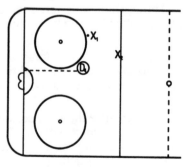

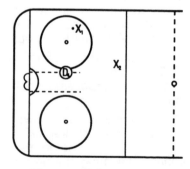

Diagram 12-7   Diagram 12-8

Basically, the goalie is responsible for the puck carrier and the defenseman for the other man (diagram 12-7). The defenseman remains on his backup line and plays for the possible pass by X1 to X2. He also tries to force the puck carrier to shooting from a poor angle.

The defenseman must back up simultaneously with the puck carrier so that the puck carrier is unable to cut behind him to the goal (diagram 12-8).

If the puck carrier (X1) cuts in front of the goal net, then the defenseman (D) must play him while the goalie prepares for a possible shot from the slot by X2. The back-checker picks up the slot man (X2).

The defenseman (D) cannot play both men, so he must play the percentages by keeping X2 well out of the slot, while also keeping X1 from cutting in behind him, into the slot area close to the goal. If X1 passes to X2 as he is making his cut to the goal, then the goaltender has time to move out of the crease to cut the angle of the shot. If the goaltender does not know what his defenseman (D) is going to do, or who he covers, then the goalie must play both forwards. In this case, the goalie cannot move out of the goal because he does not know if D will stop X1. This makes the goalie's reaction to a shot by X2 in the slot hesitant or late.

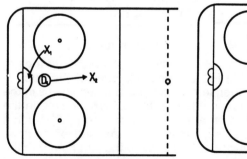
Diagram 12-9

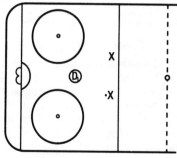
Diagram 12-10

The defenseman (diagram 12-9) should not try to cover both forwards. If he tries to go to both forwards (puck chasing) he ends up covering no one and the goalie is left with confusion in trying to stop both attackers.

Frequently, the defenseman rushes the slot man, who is able to get the puck away before the defenseman gets to him. This places the defenseman between the two attackers and covering neither one. This rush by the defenseman often results in a good screen on his goaltender, while the attacking wing (X1) positions himself in front of the goal for a tip-in, screen or rebound.

If both attackers are coming down the middle (diagram 12-10), the strategy is much the same. The defenseman stays in the slot area, leaving the area outside the slot open for the shot. Again, this is playing the percentages of having an opponent shoot from a bad angle.

THREE-ON-ONE – DEFENSIVE

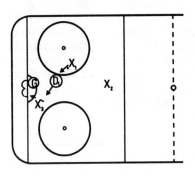 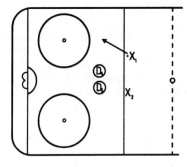

Diagram 12-11   Diagram 12-12

The defenseman (diagram 12-11) plays the slot area and tries to force the puck to the side for a poor angle shot. If the puck is already to the side, the defenseman uses his backup line as in the two-on-one. The defenseman must try to position himself on the backup line in order to cut off a pass to the far wing (X3). Such a pass forces the goalie to a long move to the other side of the goal. If the puck carrier (X1) was forced to pass to the slot man (X2) the goalie would have a short move with more time to move out and reduce the angle.

If a back-checker is present, he should cover X3 because he is deep in the slot area with an open net facing him. X3 has a higher percentage of scoring because he is deep in the slot, while X2 is well away from the goal.

TWO-ON-TWO – DEFENSIVE

The two-on-two can be a one-on-one with each defenseman (diagram 12-12). The near defenseman (D4) forces the puck carrier to the side and out of the slot area. The other defenseman (D5) covers his man (X2) and also watches for a possible pass. The back-checker plays the slot area for a rebound, pass or to pick up a late attacker.

If both attackers (X1 and X2) shift to the side (diagram 12-13) to set up a two-on-one with D4, then D5 shifts over to cover his check (X2). If a back-checker is present he takes X2, while D5 moves to his slot coverage in front of the goal.

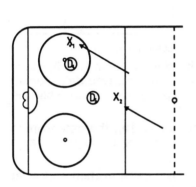   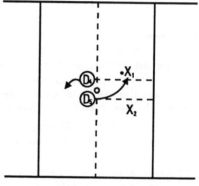

Diagram 12-13   *Diagram 12-14*

Often in a two-on-two, the defenseman can be more aggressive in attacking the attackers (diagram 12-14).

The far defenseman (D5) moves forward to angle the puck carrier (X1) to the boards. D5 plays the body and is often capable of giving a good body check. D4 can pick up the puck on this play.

Note the positioning of defensemen D4 and D5 (diagram 12-14). They are inside their checks and not facing them even up. The defensemen are on their backup line. By being inside their checks, they are helping force the play to the side.

The back-checker moves into the slot area and picks up the puck or winger, depending on the situation.

ONE-ON-TWO – DEFENSIVE

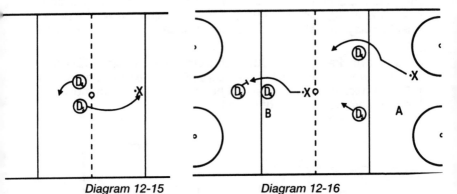

Diagram 12-15   Diagram 12-16

This is an aggressive or forcing situation (diagram 12-15), and is played like the previous two-on-two situation. One defenseman (D5) plays the puck carrier's body and body checks him, while the other defenseman (D4) plays the puck.

In the one-on-two situation (diagram 12-16), the defensemen should move towards a tandem position rather than a parallel system.

Diagram A (diagram 12-16) shows a parallel system and what happens when one defenseman is beat by the puck carrier who skates around him. Notice how D5 must chase the puck carrier because there is no backup strategy.

Diagram B (diagram 12-16) shows the tandem position of the defensemen. D5 is the back up to the play and is in position to play the puck carrier if the puck carrier moves around the first defenseman (D4).

THREE-ON-TWO – DEFENSIVE

When the puck carrier is in the middle (diagram 12-17), the defensemen maintain their back up line and force the shot or pass from well away from the goal or from a poor angle.

If the wing has the puck (diagram 12-18), the near defenseman (D4) plays him as a two-on-one situation with the emphasis on the puck carrier (X1). The far defenseman (D5) also plays a two-on-one with X2 and X3, with the emphasis on X3. As explained in the three-on-one situation, if the far wing (X3) is left open, he usually has an open net to shoot at because the goalie has the long move to the far goal post. The back-checker plays the slot man (X2).

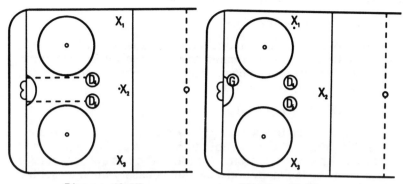

Diagram 12-17   Diagram 12-18

One of the most common problems in defending against the three-on-two is for the far defenseman (diagram 12-19) to try and cover two men at the same time, thus covering no one.

D5 is trying to cover X3 and X2 at the same time and the result is an ineffective defense against both attackers. Remember, one cannot be in two places at the same time. D5 should cover X3 who has the open net to shoot at if he gets the puck. X3 can also be an effective screen to the goaltender because he is in position for a tip-in or rebound. X2 is the goaltender's man. If X2 gets the puck, the goalie has time to move out of the crease to reduce the angle of X2's shot. As previously mentioned, if X3 gets the puck, the goalie has a long move to the far post and little chance of stopping the quick shot by X3.

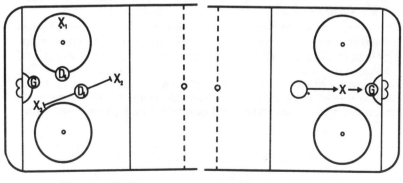

Diagram 12-19   Diagram 12-20

Basic Team Strategies – Offensive

ONE-ON-ZERO – OFFENSIVE

This is a breakaway on the goaltender (diagram 12-20). Perhaps the main strategy is not to panic and rush the the shot attempt. The attacker must remain calm and make the goaltender commit himself by making the first move.

TWO-ON-ZERO – OFFENSIVE

This is a two-man breakaway (diagram 12-21). Usually, the puck carrier (W1) draws the goaltender to one side of the goal net and uses a quick pass to this teammate (W2), who has the open net for a shot. Don't be too fancy and make unnecessary when presented with this golden scoring opportunity.

ONE-ON-ONE – OFFENSIVE

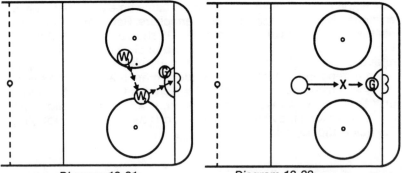

Diagram 12-21   Diagram 12-22

It is very difficult to beat, or get around a good defenseman during a one-on-one situation (diagram 12-22). Usually, the best strategy is to use the fake shot and dekes to move the defenseman into position so that he can be used as a screen for a shot on goal. The puck carrier must maintain his position in the slot and not let himself be forced from that area, unless he plans to drift in order to give a teammate time to get into position for a two-on-one advantage.

TWO-ON-ONE – OFFENSIVE

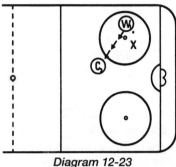 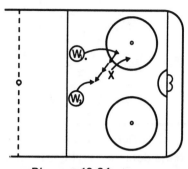

Diagram 12-23   *Diagram 12-24*

The winger (diagram 12-23) carries the puck in wide and deep, and then breaks for the goal net. The centerman maintains the slot but hangs back. If the puck carrier (W1) cannot make it to the goal, he passes back to C3.

W1 tries to draw X towards him to help open the slot area for C3.

If W1 passes to C3, then he must continue to the goal for a screen, tip-in, pass or rebound.

If the play is down the middle (diagram 12-24), the same basic strategy is employed. The puck carrier (W1) drifts to the side to pull the defenseman with him. This should open the area for his teammate (W2). Once the defenseman (X) leaves W2 open, W1 passes back to W2 in the slot. In this strategy, the puck carrier plays the role of the winger (breaks wide), and the non-puck carrier becomes the centerman (high in the slot) and slows down for the pass back play.

A variation of the two-on-one play is the crisscross pattern (diagram 12-25). This pattern can be complicated but it can also be effective if executed in a precise manner. The puck carrier crosses in front of his teammate and draws the defender (X) with him. Once X is going with W1 and the slot is open, W1 passes back (or across) to W2. It is important for W1 to wait until X moves with him before he makes the pass. If W1 passes too soon, the defender has a chance to redirect his movement to prevent the pass. Timing is crucial to this play. Faulty execution of the crisscross play just creates confusion among teammates and fails to deceive the defender.

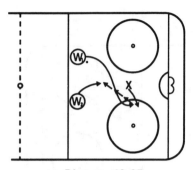   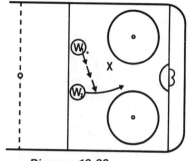

Diagram 12-25   *Diagram 12-26*

If the defenseman (X) is lined up straight on puck carrier W1 (diagram 12-26), the non-puck carrier breaks for the goal and receives a pass from the puck carrier (W1).The puck carrier (W1) hangs back for a possible return pass in the event the defender is able to move over and cover W2.

A common mistake on the two-on-one is for the two attackers to move too close together (diagram 12-27). This closeness makes it easier for the defender (X) to cover both attackers. Also, C3 is not in the slot and has a poor angle for a shot if he does get the puck.

Another common mistake is the lack of triangulation by the attackers (diagram 12-28). W1 and W2 form a straight line with the defender (X). This means the puck carrier must pass through X in order to pass the puck to his teammate (W2). Notice how W2 would be open for a pass if he positioned himself at the dotted line of triangulation.

THREE-ON-ONE – OFFENSIVE

The strategy (diagram 12-29) is to get the puck to W1 and pull the defenseman over to W1. The goalie also has to move to cover W1 for a possible shot. W2 is the far winger and he positions himself off the far goal post so that a quick pass to him will provide an open net to shoot at.

W1 and C3 play the two-on-one situation on the puck side to help open the slot area for W2. Note the triangulation of the three attackers. This gives the puck carrier (W1) an alternative if he cannot get the puck to his far winger (W2).

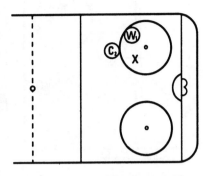

Diagram 12-27   *Diagram 12-28*

TWO-ON-TWO – OFFENSIVE

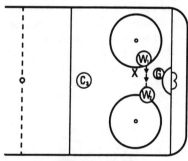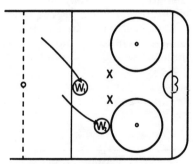

Diagram 12-29   *Diagram 12-30*

The attackers (diagram 12-30) can shift to the side, if they are not already to the side to set up the two-on-one against one of the defensemen. If the attackers stay in the middle, they will have to contend with a one-on-one situation with each attacker. Any of the two-on-one plays can be utilized.

Sometimes, the 2 on 1 criss-cross can be effective if the attackers are coming down the center ice area (diagram 12-31). The puck carrier W1 cuts over in front of W2 and pulls X2 with him. Once X2 is moving with W1, W1 passes to W2.

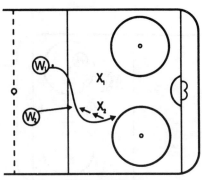

Diagram 12-31

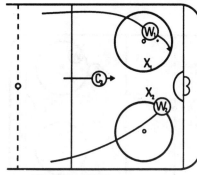

Diagram 12-32

THREE ON TWO - OFFENSIVE

The wing W1 (diagram 12-32) carries the puck over the blue line and sets up the 2 on 1 with his centerman against the near defenseman X1. The far winger breaks for the goal net.

If a back-checker is on the centerman during the three-on-two rush (diagram 12-33), then the centerman breaks for the goal net while the far wing moves over to take the slot position. The far winger is the key to this play. As the attack progresses, the far wing must read the play. If he sees his centerman breaking for the goal net because of a back-checker, then he must cut over to the slot position.

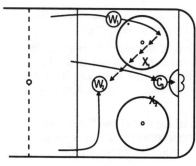

Diagram 12-33

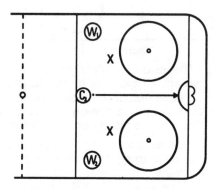

Diagram 12-34

This strategy helps to shake loose a back-checker, or pull the back-checker towards the goal net. This opens the slot area for the far wing man. The three attackers still maintain good triangulation and positional play with a man (C3) in front of the goal and a wing man (W2) high in the slot for a shot or back-checking

If the defensemen are playing too wide (diagram 12-34), the centerman (C3) may have an opening straight to the goal net.

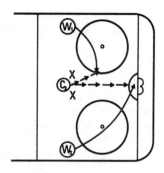

Diagram 12-35

If the defensemen are high and close together, and not moving back too fast (diagram 12-35), then fast breaking wingers can break around the defense and take a soft pass from the centerman or play the center's shot on goal.

XIII. The Breakout Play

The breakout play may well be the most important play in hockey. A hockey team must be able to break out of its own end in order to go on the attack. Naturally, if a team cannot break out of its defensive zone, it will be difficult to score.

The Breakout Play from Behind the Goal Net

Once positive possession of the puck is gained in the defensive zone, the players move to their break out positions. Very often possession is gained behind the goal net, or the puck is passed behind the net to organize the breakout play. The breakout play must be simple, yet have variety and diversity. The players must have alternative plays if their first play choice is blocked. Alternative plays should be in a systematic order so that each player knows what is happening and what is supposed to happen next. This keeps the team thinking as a unit.

The key to the breakout play is in positive puck possession. The players must not move to their break out positions until the team has positive control of the puck. If players move prematurely, they may be leaving their checks open for a quick scoring opportunity if the opposition gains puck control.

A good breakout play will move the puck out quickly and trap some of the opposing team's fore-checkers deep in the end zone. Trapping puts the fore-checkers in position to be late in their back-checking duties. To trap the fore-checkers, the breakout players must position themselves to be able to break out quickly, as well as play defense if puck possession is lost. If the forwards are deep in the end zone, they will provide good protection if puck possession is lost, and also be in position for a quick pass. By being too deep in the end zone, players may have difficulty breaking out, as well as trapping the opposition deep in the end zone.

If the forwards are placed well up to the blue line, they can break out quickly, although they may offer less protection, defensively. Passing to forwards in such a position is difficult and can be dangerous, but it can also be so very effective.

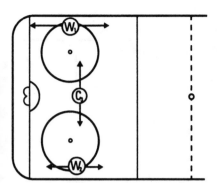

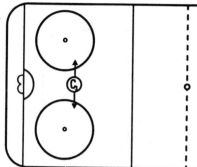

Diagram 13-1   Diagram 13-2

The positioning of W1, W2 and C3 (diagram 13-1) will depend on the situation and the opposition. SThe opponent's positioning will force W1, W2, and C3 to move in deep or play closer to the blue line. Regardless of the opponent's positioning, they are still in their basic position. Notice how the wings move wide to the boards during a breakout play. This opens the attack and gives the defensive team more area to cover.

The players must not break out before the puck carrier is ready. Wingers that break too soon will kill the attack. A good rule to follow is to wait for the puck carrier to lift his head and indicate he is ready to advance.

The first choice on the breakout play is to pass to the centerman in the mid-ice area. The centerman should skate back and forth (diagram 13-2), parallel to the blue line and wait for a pass. He must be careful if skating vertically to the blue line because he will have to receive a pass while looking over his shoulder. Besides being dangerous, it is difficult to pass accurately under such conditions.

If the center man is outside the blue line (diagram 13-3), he should cross the blue line to the side so that he can break parallel to the blue line to receive the pass.

If the mid-ice area is too congested (diagram 13-4) then the centerman will go behind the goal net to help organize the breakout. He should proceed at about half to three-quarter speed. While going behind the goal net, the centerman must look to the area around the goal net for opposition fore-checkers so he can decide on two alternatives 1) taking the puck, or 2) leaving the puck with the defenseman.

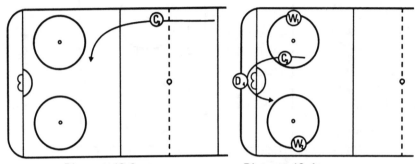

Diagram 13-3   Diagram 13-4

If the centerman takes the puck because it is clear of fore-check-ers in front of the goal, he should immediately cut up the middle, between his wingers.

If the centerman (diagram 13-5) takes the puck and soon finds that he is blocked by a fore-checker, he simply drops the puck back to the trailing defenseman or, if possible, makes a quick pass to the wing.

If the centerman (diagram 13-6) leaves the puck for the defenseman, because the center ice lane is blocked by a fore-checker, he will proceed wide to the corner, and the winger on his side will break into the center area to become the centerman. The winger must break straight across and parallel to the blue line. The defenseman can pass to the centerman (C3) or to the breaking winger (W2). It is possible that the defenseman may even move the puck to the other side to pass to the far winger who may be open.

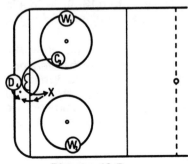
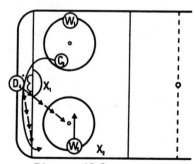

Diagram 13-5   Diagram 13-6

This same play can be used by the winger to leave his check on the boards. If the fore-checker (X2) moves with W2, then C3 has clear access out of the end zone and D4 can give him the pass.

Simplified, the rules are as follows:

1. Do not break too soon. Wait until ready.
2. Pass to the centerman in the mid-ice area.
3. If the centerman has to go behind the goal net, he will either 1) take the puck, or 2) leave the puck with the defenseman.
4. If the centerman takes the puck, he breaks up the middle. If the centerman leaves the puck, he goes wide to the corner while the winger breaks to the center.

This breakout play has a consistency and a sequence when studying player movement. The diversity and variety creates several passing options.

XIV. The Three-Two System

This is the system employed by most present-day hockey teams in North America. Its name is derived from the formation of three forwards and two defensemen. Although this formation may alter in the defensive and offensive end zones, the basic strategy is to have the three forwards work as a separate unit from the two defensemen. This system can be effective, despite the change in checks in each end zone. The change in checks is the result of the winger covering the opposition's winger, but ends up covering the defenseman in the end zones. Unfortunately, this switching from winger coverage to defenseman coverage can create problems.

The three-two system contains strong zone coverage with some man-to-man coverage.

Defensive End Zone Play

The end zone coverage has several patterns. They are:

1. Winger in puck corner and the centerman on the point (opposing defenseman).
2. Both wings on the points.
3. First forward in the corner, second forward on the point.
4. One man covering both points.

The following diagrams will clarify these patterns.

WINGER IN PUCK CORNER AND CENTER ON NEAR POINT

Near winger W2 (diagram 14-1) goes into the corner to help defenseman D5 gain puck possession. Centerman C3 stays back to cover point LD. The far winger (W1) is high in the slot, covering point RD and helping defenseman D4 with slot coverage. The strategy between the near defenseman and the near winger in gaining puck possession is for the first player to play the man and the second player to get the puck.

Once puck possession is gained (diagram 14-2), the players move to their break out positions. The wings move to the boards while the centerman (C3) loops into the center area for the break out pass. Defenseman (D4) remains in front of the goal net if he feels it is not safe to leave the slot area. D4 must not leave the slot area unless a teammate has possession of the puck. When it is safe, D4 can go behind the goal or into the far corner to receive a pass from D5. One advantage of this end zone formation is that the wings are to the boards and the centerman is positioned in the center of the ice for the breakout. The centerman plays close to the boards so that he can play the puck if it is banged up the boards, and he also has a good angle to loop into center ice for the breakout.

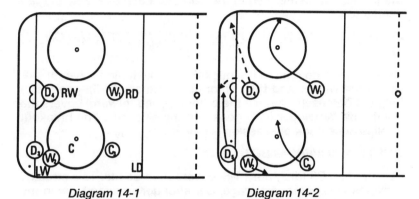

Diagram 14-1   *Diagram 14-2*

For the breakout (diagram 14-3), D5 can pass to D4, W1, W2, and C3 if he is able to gain possession behind the goal net. If he is not able to get behind the goal net, then he can make a breakout pass before he gets behind the net. If D4 is alert, he can often take the pass by skating into the corner.

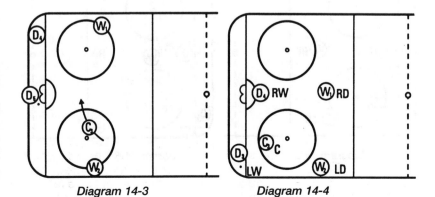

Diagram 14-3   *Diagram 14-4*

BOTH WINGS ON THE POINT

This strategy (diagram 14-4) is similar to the previous one, except the centerman C3 goes into the corner to help the defenseman gain puck possession. Notice how in most cases C3 will position himself a little more to the net while backing up his defenseman (D5). The same corner play strategy applies in that the defenseman plays the man and the centerman picks up the puck. When puck possession is gained, the breakout play is executed. An advantage of this system is in the simplicity of execution – wingers on the points and centermen in the corners. Each has a clearly defined role.

FIRST FORWARD IN THE CORNER, SECOND FORWARD ON THE POINT

The player who gets to the puck the quickest (first forward), between the winger and the centerman (diagram 14-5), goes in to help the defenseman while the other (second forward) covers the point. The far winger (W1) goes into the slot area. The breakout applies once puck possession is gained.

ONE MAN COVERING BOTH POINTS

Centerman C3 (diagram 14-6) covers both points. This strategy provides weak point coverage, but stronger coverage low in the slot, around the goal mouth, and in the puck corner. This may be dangerous if the opposition has strong point play. When puck possession is gained, then the players move to the breakout play.

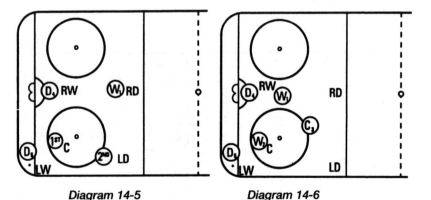

Diagram 14-5   *Diagram 14-6*

Offensive End Zone Play

Offensive end zone play is based on triangulation of the three forwards. The three systems are:

1. Winger in the corner.

2. Center in the corner.

3. First in the corner, second back-up.

WINGER IN THE CORNER

Winger W1 (diagram 14-7) plays the corner with centerman C3 backing him up. Winger W1 plays the man while centerman C3 picks up the puck. The far winger (W2) plays the slot. The positioning of C3 will vary according to the opposition. C3 can play tight to W1 to provide two men on the puck (position 1), or he can play back a little more (position 2) to give only one man on the puck. C3 in the second position, (2) gives extra backchecking potential as well as position to attack the corner or the goal net.

CENTERMAN IN THE CORNER

The centerman (C3) in the corner (diagram 14-8) utilizes the same strategy as previously outlined. An advantage of this system is that the two wingers (W1 and W2) are in position to backcheck.

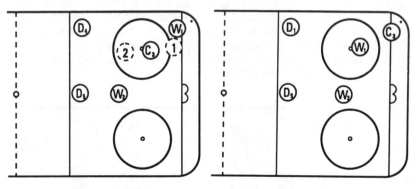

Diagram 14-7   *Diagram 14-8*

FIRST IN THE CORNER, SECOND BACK-UP

Once again the strategy is the same (diagram 14-9), except that the player who can get to the puck first (1) goes into the corner and the second player (2) plays backup. The far winger covers the slot.

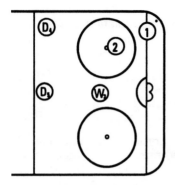

Diagram 14-9

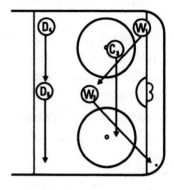

Diagram 14-10

PLAYER MOVEMENT WHEN THE PUCK MOVES TO OTHER CORNER

When the puck moves quickly to the other corner (diagram 14-10), the following rotation occurs. The slotman (W2) goes to the puck corner while the back-up man (C3) moves over to back up W2. The far winger (W1) moves to the slot position. This rotation leaves the wings to their own side of the ice. The defensemen simply shift with the puck.

If the centerman C3 is in the corner (diagram 14-11) and the coach does not desire to have his wing move over to the other side of the ice to back up the corner, he can use the following pattern. The wing (W1) moves to the slot position, while the centerman (C3) cuts across to take his backup with W2. The weakness in this system is that it takes a little longer for C3 to be in back up position. The defensemen shift with the puck.

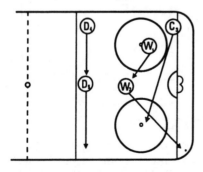

Diagram 14-11

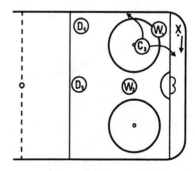

Diagram 14-12

If opponent X gains puck possession (diagram 14-12) and escapes from W1, then the back up man (C3) moves in to play the puck carrier. The defensemen (D4 and D5) must be alert for the quick breakout pass by the opposition.

If the puck is carried behind the goal net by opponent X1, then the players use the following strategy (diagram 14-13). W1 chases the puck carrier and forces him towards the goal net, while C3 angles the puck carrier to go behind the goal net. If C3 can stop the puck carrier before he gets behind the goal net then C3 should do so. Otherwise, C3 continues in front of the goal net to be the back up man on the other side. W2 cuts in off the goal net to pick up the puck carrier. W2 must time his move precisely with the puck carrier. If W2 moves too slow, then the puck carrier will skate by him, and if W2 moves too fast, then the puck carrier cuts behind W2 and breaks out. The defensemen (D4 and D5) shift with the play. If the puck carrier (X1) stops behind the goal net, then the following two plays (diagram 14 and diagram 15) will be effective.

If the puck carrier (X1) stops behind the goal (diagram 14-14), then W2 can go behind the goal net to defend him, while C3 continues to the boards to cover the opposition's wing. When C3 sees W2 definitely going behind the goal net, then that is his key to cover the far wing (X3). W1 loops around to pick up his check (X2). The defense shift with the play.

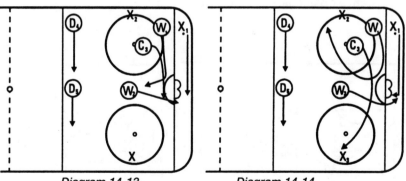

Diagram 14-13   Diagram 14-14

If W2 is unable to play the puck carrier (X1) effectively behind the goal net (diagram 14-15), W2 can leave him for C3, who stops in front of the net to play the puck carrier (X1). If C3 sees that W2 does not go behind the goal net, then C3 must remain in front of the goal net to play the puck carrier (X1). W2 continues his pattern to the boards to pick up his check (X3). W1 also loops around to pick his check (X2). The defense shifts with the play.

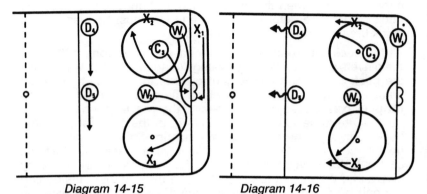

Diagram 14-15   Diagram 14-16

With this offensive end zone strategy, the wings can break off for back-checking duties or, as in diagram 14-16, the back-up man (C3) and the far winger (W2) peel off for back-checking duties.

In choosing a pattern for defensive end zone play (diagram 14-17), the strategy must coordinate with the offensive end zone play so that back-checking duties do not cause confusion in the defensive end zone. Confusion about back-checking duties may occur when the wing and center switch duties while fore-checking. When the back-checking moves into the defensive end zone there may be confusion as to when the wing and center should return to their respective positions.

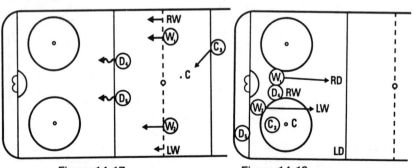

Figure 14-17   Figure 14-18

Face-off Positions

DEFENSIVE END ZONE FACE-OFF

Diagram 14-18 is the standard face-off formation. W1 covers RD. W2 covers LW wherever LW is positioned. D4 is on the face-off circle to cover RW and still be in the slot area. If C3 gets the draw to D5, D5 goes behind the goal net to set up the breakout play. If the situation presents itself, D5 can break up the boards towards LD. In most cases, LD will back out of the end zone if the play comes towards him. If D5 cannot get by LD, he can pass the puck off the boards into the neutral ice area.

OFFENSIVE END ZONE FACE-OFF

Diagram 14-19 is the standard face-off formation.

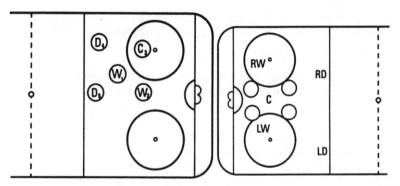

Figure 14-19   *Figure 14-20*

Penalty Killing - The Box Formation

DEFENSIVE END ZONE – ONE MAN SHORT

The Box (diagram 14-20) is the standard penalty killing formation. The main purpose of this strategy is to keep the puck to the outside and away from the slot area.

When the puck is in the corner (diagram 14-21), the near defenseman (D5) moves out, but does not attack the puck unless he is able to gain positive possession. The main strategy of D5 is to keep LW in the corner, or force him to pass. D5 must not let LW get by him and into the slot area. The opposition's slot man (C) is covered by W1. W1 is the farthest man from the puck.

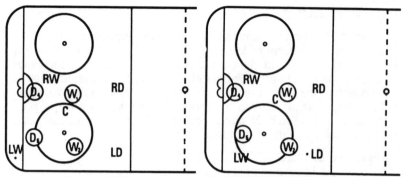

Figure 14-21   Figure 14-22

If the opposition's pointman LD has the puck (diagram 14-22), he is covered by W2 who must remain between LD and the goal. The slotman (C) is covered by W1.

If LD passes to RD (diagram 14-23), then W1 moves out to cover RD, and W2 moves into the slot against C. D5 adjusts accordingly.

DEFENSIVE END ZONE – TWO MEN SHORT

Diagram 14-24 is the basic triangle system. C3 covers both points while the defense are responsible for the goal net area.

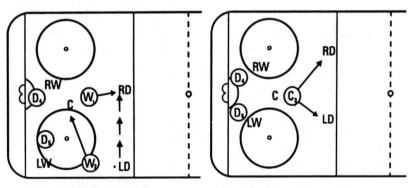

Figure 14-23   Figure 14-24

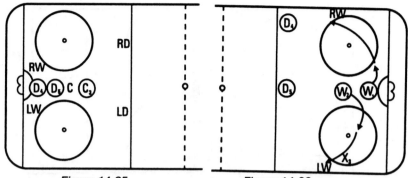

Figure 14-25   Figure 14-26

Another system for the two men short situation is the tandem formation (diagram 14-25). This formation is to cover the slot and force the shots from a poor angle. The three defenders are in a straight line to give strong slot coverage, especially against C. C3 covers both points while D4 and D5 shift as necessary to the two most dangerous men between RW, C and LW.

FORE-CHECKING – ONE MAN SHORT

Player W1 (diagram 14-26), the first fore-checker, fore-checks and peels off to one wing. W2, the backup to W1, goes to the side opposite W1. Each will pick up a wing to back-check.

Another fore-checking strategy (diagram 14-27) is to have the forwards (W1 and W2) go to the opposition's wings and leave the center ice lane open. Back-checking begins from this positioning. The reasoning for this strategy is because rarely is a fore-checker able to do much damage against a power breakout play, so why not let the opposition get started? By immediately moving to cover their respective players, there is less chance of a fore-checker getting caught or trapped in the end zone. When a fore-checker is trapped in the end zone, the opposition is breaking out against only three defenders.

BACK-CHECKING – ONE MAN SHORT

The back-checkers (diagram 14-28) are needed so that the defensemen (D4 and D5) can "stand-up" in front of the blue line to force the attack at the blue line. When the four defenders are able to force the play at the blue line, the opposition has difficulty against the wall of defenders.

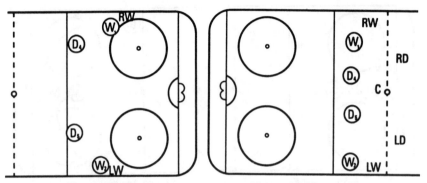

Figure 14-27   *Figure 14-28*

The Power Play

DEFENSIVE END ZONE – POWER PLAY

In most cases, the breakout play (outlined in Chapter 11) will originate behind the goal net as in diagram 14-29. In most cases, the
defenseman (D5), moves out to the wing (W1) from in front of the
goal net, and skates with the wing up the ice but slightly behind
the wing. By staying slightly behind the wing, the puck carrier is
able to pass to the wing or the breaking defenseman (D5). With the
defenseman breaking with the winger, the attack has a stronger
chance of penetrating to the opposition's goal. The defenseman
(D4), behind the goal net, trails the play as the back up. If desired,
it is possible to have D4 breakup the side opposite to the other
defenseman (D5) for two strong sides to the attack.

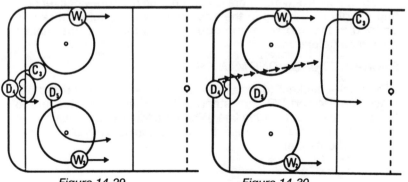

Figure 14-29   *Figure 14-30*

An effective and quick breakout (diagram 14-30) is sometimes supposed to have the centerman (C3) delay his return to the defensive end zone so that he can cut parallel to the blue line and receive a long pass from D4. This play is extremely effective in trapping an opposition's fore-checker deep in the end zone.

OFFENSIVE END ZONE – POWER PLAY

Diagram 14-31 is the standard power play formation. Various patterns can be developed by passing the puck to set up two-on-one situations by shifting C3 to various corners of the box and slot area.

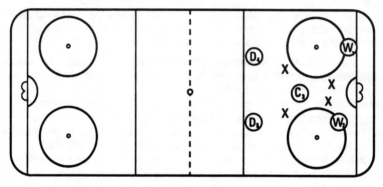

Diagram 14-31

XV. Drills

The following drills are just a sample of what the coach can utilize. The drills can be altered to meet the teams needs. Many of the drills can be made more complex and demanding by the addition of other skills and time limits. The coach, in picking and devising his drills, must design his drills for game situations. The use of a drill must be constantly evaluated. Is the drill meeting the needs of the team? Is the drill progressing to meet the improvement of the players? Is the drill getting boring? Is any learning taking place from the drill? These questions, and more, must be answered by the coach and perhaps even by the players.

It is important to remember that drills are just drills. The coach and player must use the drills to develop the game skills and patterns. The drill must fit into the team strategy. The drill must be executed in the same precise manner as during game conditions. Some teams are very good at performing drills, but fail to see how it fits into the game strategy. Coaches make the fatal error of doing drills and then scrimmaging. Coaches must do the drill, then scrimmage to emphasize the skill or strategy under game conditions, and then practice the drill again and scrimmage again. This process must be repeated as often as necessary until the players understand how the drill will help them during the game.

Skating

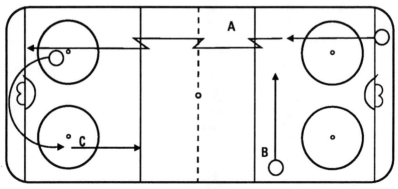

Diagram 15-1

STOP AND START (DIAGRAM 15-1)

The stop and start drill can be performed lengthwise, with stop and starts on the blue and red lines (A); sideways, with stop and starts at each side (B); or while skating around the rink, with stop and starts at the blue and red lines (C).

The stop and starts can be performed to the whistle instead of at the lines. Performing to the whistle means the players have no forewarning of when to stop or start. These drills should be performed with backward and forward skating.

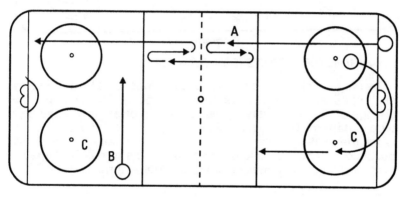

Diagram 15-2

QUICK TURNABOUT (DIAGRAM 15-2)

The quick turnabout drill is performed lengthwise, with the turnabouts or 180 degree changes of direction at the lines (A); sideways, with turnabouts at the boards (B); or while skating around the rink (C). The turnabouts can also be executed to the whistle and with forward and backward skating.

CROSSOVER (DIAGRAM 15-3)

The figure eight skating pattern is good practice for the crossover skating stride. The tightness of the turn can easily be regulated by the size of the space. Figure eights around the rink and behind the nets give a large turn (A), while figure eights between the blue lines is much smaller and require tighter turns (B). C and D can also be used for variety.

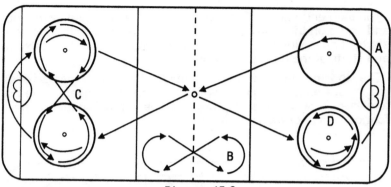

Diagram 15-3

CHANGING DIRECTIONS (DIAGRAM 15-4)

The diagram shows the change of directions to be 90 degrees by skating the square. If desired, the use of obstacles can make the change of directions vary by using triangle patterns or any other type of pattern. The main emphasis in the change of direction drill is for the skater to make the change of direction as quickly as possible with no rounding of the corner. If the turn is 90 degrees, then the skater must make a sharp 90 degree turn.

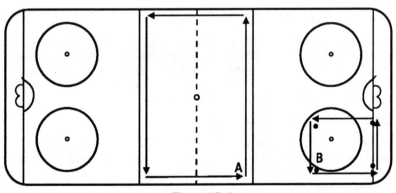

Figure 15-4

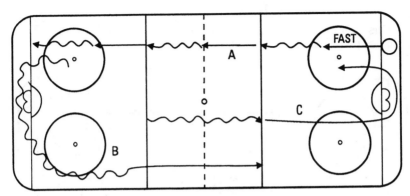

Diagram 15-5

QUICK BREAKS (DIAGRAM 15-5)

Quick breaks can be performed at the blue lines (A); between the blue lines (B); or around the goal nets (C). This drill can also be performed by breaking to the whistle. An interesting aspect to this drill is to do push-ups after each quick break. Another method closer to game conditions is to skate at half speed and on the whistle or blue lines, have the skaters do five push-ups, get up and break down the ice as quickly as possible. This is a game condition drill that simulates what it takes to get back into a play after being knocked down onto the ice.

SCOOTING (DIAGRAM 15-6)

Almost any pattern can be used for this drill. The diagram uses the lines as a guide, and the player switches scooting legs with each change of direction.

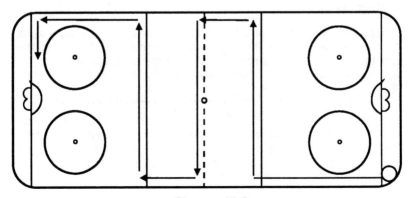

Diagram 15-6

PIVOTING (DIAGRAM 15-7)

This drill can be performed lengthwise or around the rink. The player pivots at the various lines or to the whistle.

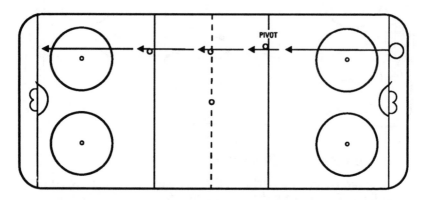

Diagram 15-7

CHANGE OF PACE (DIAGRAM 15-8)

This drill can be performed lengthwise, or around the rink with the change of pace at the lines or to the whistle.

LATERAL MOBILITY (DIAGRAM 15-9)

The players follow the leader's movements or arm signals (A), or imitates the lateral action of a partner (B). In (C), the player's body faces the end of the rink throughout the drill while he moves up the boards and sideways along the lines.

FORWARD TO BACKWARD TO FORWARD, ETC.
(DIAGRAM 15-10)

The player skates forward from the blue line to the red line, stops, skates backward to the blue line, stops, and forward again to the red line, etc. (A). This can be repeated from blue line to blue line for a longer run (B). C is another pattern for the same procedure.

TANDEM PUSH AND TANDEM PULL (DIAGRAM 15-11)

In the push drill, the player pushes his partner who gives resistance with the snowplow stop (A). In the pull drill the player is pulling his partner through the use of hockey sticks (B). Again, the partner gives resistance by slightly digging the skates into the ice. This drill can also be done with backward skating.

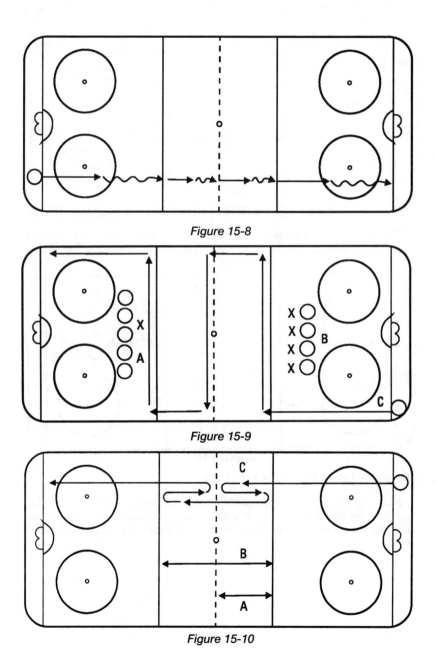

Figure 15-8

Figure 15-9

Figure 15-10

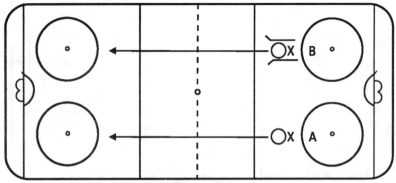

Figure 15-11

LATERAL BACKWARD SKATING FOR AGILITY (DIAGRAM 15-12)

The players move backward through a series of lateral movements, starting one after the other to avoid running into each other.

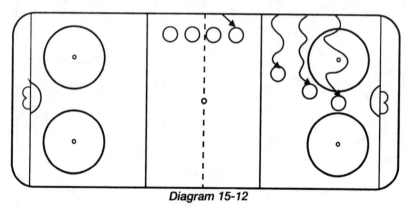

Diagram 15-12

MIRROR DRILLS (DIAGRAM 15-13)

Mirror drills develop agility, reflexes and timing. The drill can be performed by mirroring the movements of a leader (A), or a partner (B). Mirror drills are excellent when used with a puck for puck control practice.

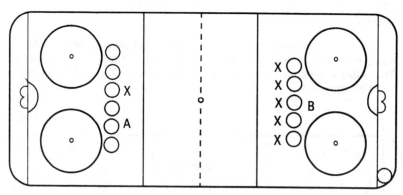

Diagram 15-13

Puck Control

STICKHANDLING

The skating drills and patterns will work well for stickhandling practice.

STATIONARY STICKHANDLING (DIAGRAM 15-14)

Diagrams A and B are examples of the different formation a leader can use. The players move to the arm signals of the leader. For variety, the players, while stickhandling, can call out the number of fingers the leader holds up. This forces the players to look up at the leader's hand and not at the puck.

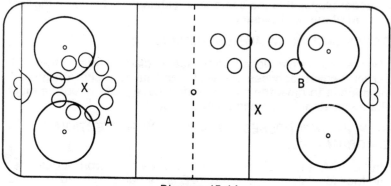

Diagram 15-14

SMALL AREA SCRIMMAGE AND "KEEP AWAY" (DIAGRAM 15-15)

The blue lines divide the rink into three small playing areas, where the puck carrier tries to keep the puck from the others in the area. This also works well with teams that stickhandle and pass with their teammates.

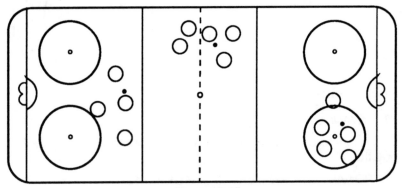

Figure 15-15

PUCK KICKS (DIAGRAM 15-16)

Pucks are placed about five feet in front of the players (A). The player breaks, takes control of the puck with his skates by kicking the puck ahead to his stick blade. This is repeated at the blue lines. Figure B is a variation in which the players control and move the puck with their feet by sliding the puck to each foot, much like a soccer player. It is the same as stickhandling, by using the feet instead of the hockey stick.

STICKHANDLING WEAVE (DIAGRAM 15-17)

Hockey sticks are placed on the ice as diagramed and the puck carrier weaves between the sticks and takes a shot on goal. A variation is to have the player in the weave pattern, but he must skate in a straight line and jump over each stick.

GAINING PUCK POSSESSION AND PUCK PROTECTION (DIAGRAM 15-18)

In figure A, the puck carrier protects the puck from a defender and tries for a shot on goal. Figure B is a scramble situation where the puck is placed behind the defender and the attacker 'X' tries

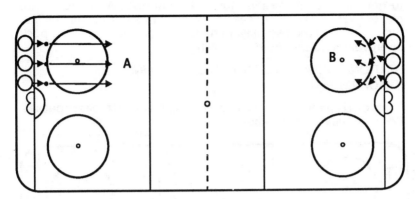

Figure 15-16

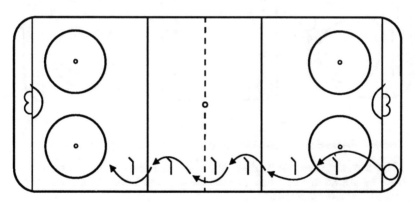

Figure 15-17

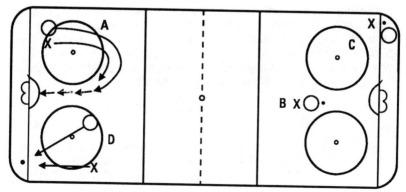

Figure 15-18

to get the puck in position for a shot on goal. At figure C, two players fight for puck possession while at D, a puck is thrown into the corner and the two players rush in to gain control of the puck or prevent the other from controlling.

STATIONARY PASSING AND PASS RECEIVING (DIAGRAM 15-19)

This drill is performed at various distances, with all types of passes, both forehand and backhand.

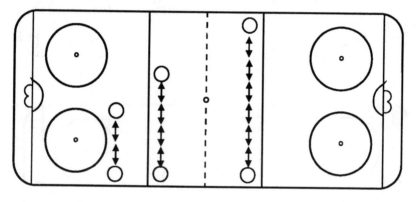

Figure 15-19

SHORT PASSES (DIAGRAM 15-20)

The players give each other short quick passes (A). In figure B, hockey sticks are used as obstacles to pass between or, for variety, to pass over the stick.

GIVE-AND-TAKE (DIAGRAM 15-21)

In the single give-and-take (A), the player passes to a player and then receives the pass back. Figure B is the double give-and-take. In this drill and other similar drills, it is best if the players do not line up in the corner for their turn. Shots on goal often end up in the corner so it can be dangerous in the corner. Therefore, players should position themselves away from the corner.

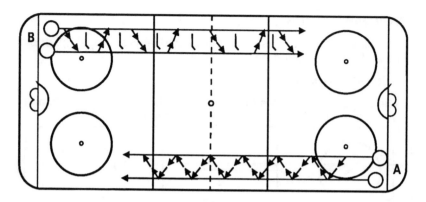

Figure 15-20

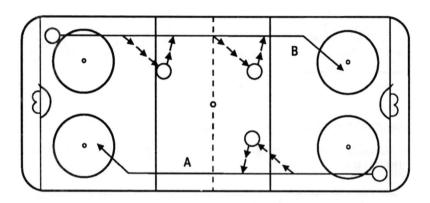

Figure 15-21

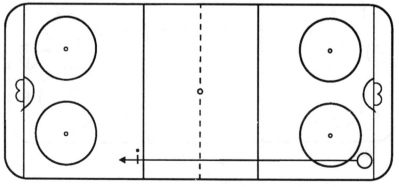

Figure 15-22

DROP PASS (DIAGRAM 15-22)

The player stickhandles down the ice and leaves (drops) the puck in a stationary position on the blue line.

PASS BACK (DIAGRAM 15-23)

The player stickhandles down the ice, crosses the blue line, and passes back so that the sliding puck on the blue line.

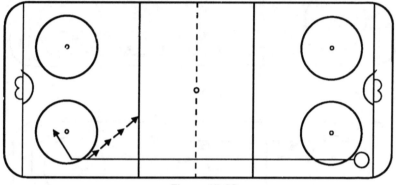

Figure 15-23

PASS BACK TO PLAYER (DIAGRAM 15-24)

The puck carrier passes back to another player who takes the shot on goal.

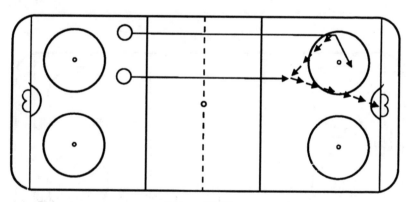

Figure 15-24

OBSTACLE PASS (DIAGRAM 15-25)

The players skate on each side of the obstacles (hockey sticks) or pass to each other between the sticks (A) and over the sticks (B).

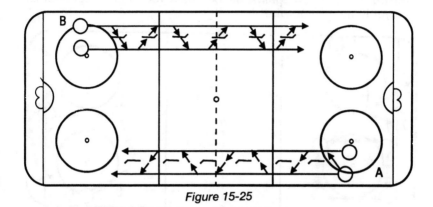

Figure 15-25

PASS RECEIVING AND QUICK SHOT (DIAGRAM 15-26)

A player breaks towards the net, receives a pass, and makes a quick shot on goal. Passes can be made from A, B, or C.

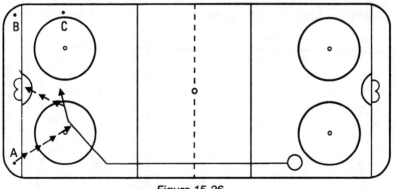

Figure 15-26

A variation is to roll the puck out on its edge, giving the shooter a chance to practice shooting the bouncing and rolling puck. The shooters should practice shooting in stride.

PASS DEFLECTION AND REBOUND PASSING (DIAGRAM 15-27)

The players keep the puck moving by taking the pass and passing in one smooth, quick motion (A). In figure B, the players do the same thing except the last man takes a shot on goal. In figure C, the puck is shot low against the boards to rebound out for another player to move in for the shot.

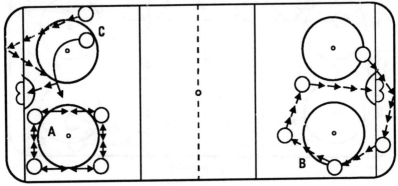

Figure 15-27

BEHIND THE BACK PASSING (DIAGRAM 15-28)

Coming down the ice, the players pass to each other with behind-the-back passes (A). In figure B, the puck carrier makes a behind-the-back pass to a man in front of the net for a shot on goal.

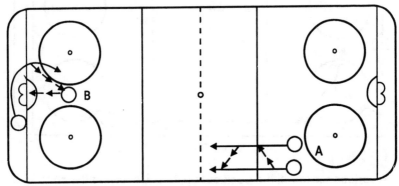

Figure 15-28

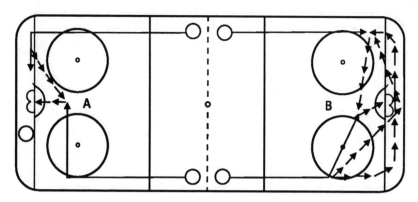

Figure 15-29

OPPOSITE WINGER PASS (DIAGRAM 15-29)

The puck carrier carries the puck into the corner and passes out to a teammate, the opposite winger, in front of the goal net for a shot on goal (A). A variation is to have the puck carrier pass to the opposite winger by passing the puck behind the net or rounding it off the boards. The opposite winger then returns the pass in front of the net for the shot on goal (B).

STATIONARY SHOOTING (DIAGRAM 15-30)

Figures A and B are different lineup positions for shots on goal. The lineup on the red line can be used to shoot at an empty net for accuracy.

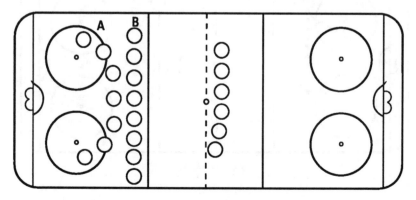

Figure 15-30

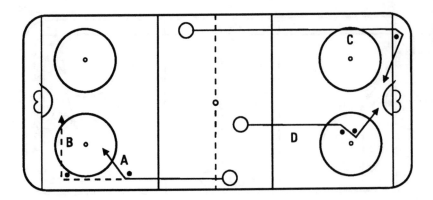

Figure 15-31

CUTTING TO THE NET AND SHOOTING (DIAGRAM 15-31)

Obstacles are placed in various positions (A, B, C and D) for the players to cut around for a shot on goal. The give-and-take drill can be used before the player takes his cut to the goal.

SPEED SHOOTING (DIAGRAM 15-32)

Pucks are arranged in a line (A, B and C). The player starts at the end of the line and moves down the line, shooting each puck as fast as possible without interruption or breaking stride.

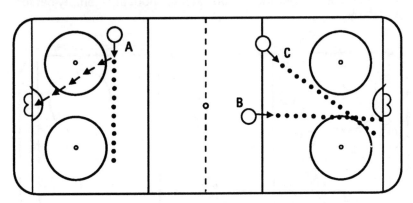

Figure 15-32

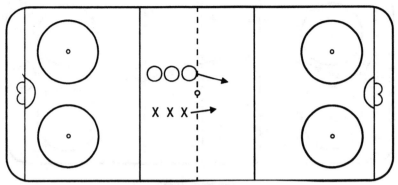

Figure 15-33

PRESSURE SHOTS (DIAGRAM 15-33)

The players form two teams. Each player gets one shot on goal. The object is to see which team can score the most goals.

SHOOTING IN STRIDE (DIAGRAM 15-34)

This drill is to give every player practice at shooting in stride. This drill can be progressed to shooting on goal. From mid-ice, the players skate to the boards and shoot the puck at the boards while skating without breaking stride to get the shot away. A variation is to place the puck well in front of the player so that the player skates full stride, picks up the puck and shoots it quickly and in stride.

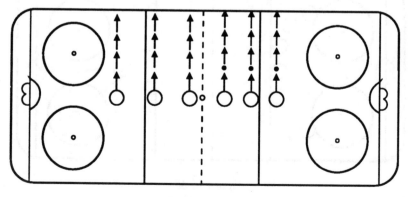

Diagram 15-34

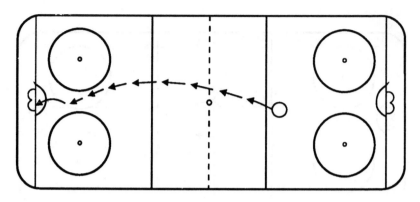

Diagram 15-35

FLIP SHOT (DIAGRAM 15-35)

The players flip the puck down the ice to land near the goal area. Variations are to place the puck fairly close to the goaltender and then try to flip the puck over a sprawling goaltender.

SCREENS AND TIP-INS (DIAGRAM 15-36)

One player positions himself in front of the goal net to screen shots and take tip-ins (A). A variation is to have a player pass to a teammate and then break in front of the goal to tip the shot and screen the goalie (B).

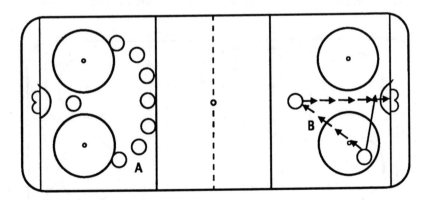

Figure 15-36

Checking

STICK-CHECKING (DIAGRAM 15-37)

One player stick checks the other stickhandling player. Players work in a limited area and practice all types of stick checks.

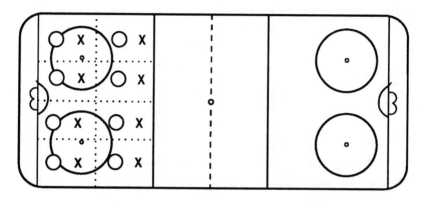

Figure 15-37

THREE LINES OF DEFENSE (DIAGRAM 15-38)

This is a one-on-one situation. The defender stops the puck carrier by using the poke check, then the body check and then the hook check.

BODY CHECKING

Defenders use hockey sticks that have the blades cut off. This forces the defenders to play the body, as their sticks aren't of much use. Many drills and scrimmages can be conducted in this manner.

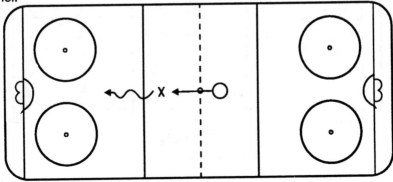

Figure 15-38

Game Situations

ONE-ON-ONE (DIAGRAM 15-39)

The puck carrier approaches from three different areas (A, B and C).

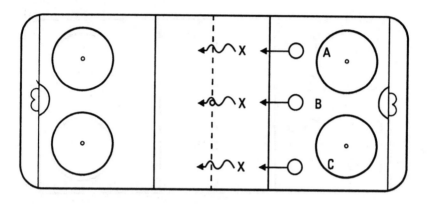

Figure 15-39

ONE-ON-TWO (DIAGRAM 15-40)

The puck carrier approaches two defensemen from three different areas (A, B and C). This drill can also be done with one defenseman and one back-checker.

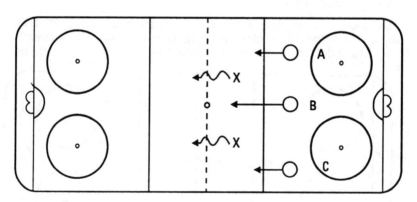

Figure 15-40

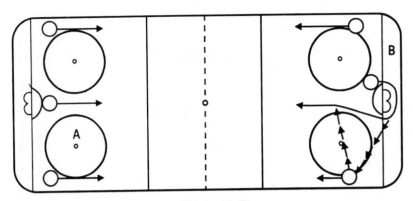

Figure 15-41

STARTING THE TWO OR THREE MAN ATTACK/RUSH (DIAGRAM 15-41)

In section A, the players line up and advance down the ice. In figure B, the centerman picks up a puck and goes around the goal net, passes to a winger and takes the pass back (give-and-go).

TWO-ON-ONE (DIAGRAM 15-42)

The approach of the attackers can be from the sides or from the middle.

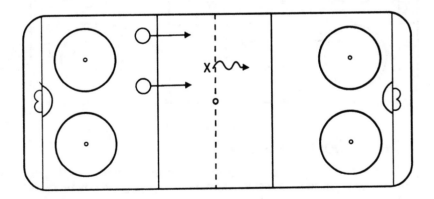

Figure 15-42

TWO-ON-TWO (DIAGRAM 15-43)

The approach can be from the side or the middle. A variation is to use one defenseman and one back-checker.

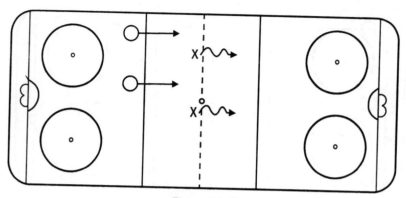

Figure 15-43

TWO-ON-THREE (DIAGRAM 15-44)

Two defensemen and one back-checker check the two attackers.

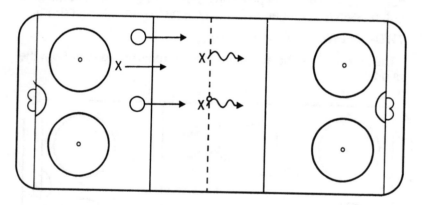

Figure 15-44

THREE-ON-NONE (DIAGRAM 15-45)

The three attackers use various passing combinations to set up a shot on goal. Good for passing, shooting and giving the goaltenders action.

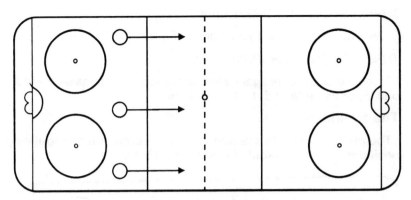

Figure 15-45

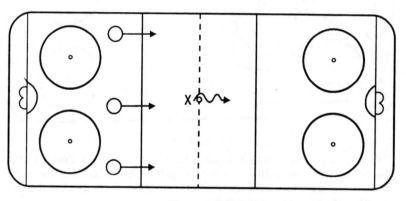

Figure 15-46

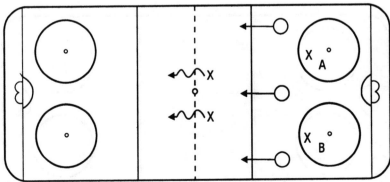

Figure 15-47

THREE-ON-ONE (DIAGRAM 15-46)

Three attackers work against one defender

THREE-ON-TWO (DIAGRAM 15-47)

Three attackers work against two defenders. Variations are to add one (A) or two (A and B) back-checkers.

The Breakout

The puck is shot into the corner and the players move to their positions for the breakout play (diagram 15-48).

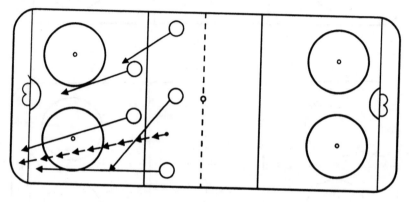

Figure 15-48

With puck possession (diagram 15-49), the players break to receive the pass. A variation is for the puck carrier to take the puck behind the goal and wait for the centerman to skate behind the net to pick up the puck or leave it.

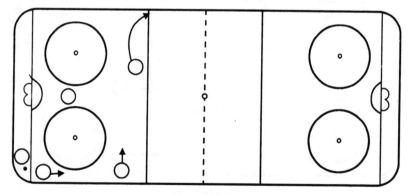

Figure 15-49

The breakout should also be practiced with one to five checkers (diagram 15-50)

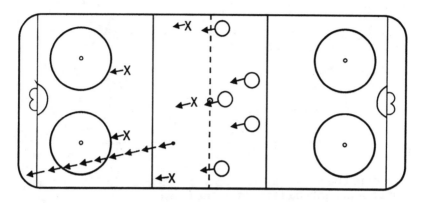

Figure 15-50

Fore-checking

In diagram 15-51 (A), the puck carrier takes the puck behind the goal net. The checker 'X' tries to prevent the puck carrier from breaking out with the puck. In figure B, the puck is shot into the corner and each player tries to gain puck possession or prevent the other from gaining possession. In figure C, the defenseman and winger team up against the fore-checker (O).

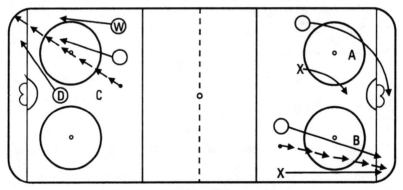

Figure 15-51

In diagram 15-52, the puck is shot into the end zone and the team sets up in fore-checking positions for a shot on goal.

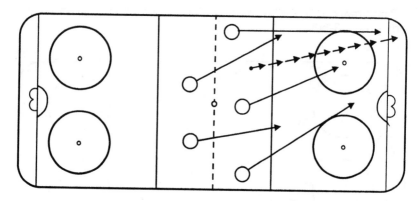

Figure 15-52

The fore-checking team has opponents (diagram 15-53). The number of opponents can vary from one to five.

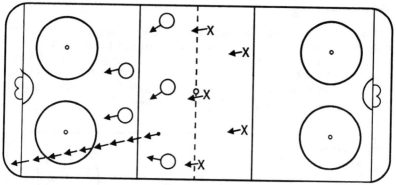

Figure 15-53

Back-checking

Many previous drills contain back-checking.

In diagram 15-54, the puck carrier breaks along the boards and the back-checker tries to prevent him from shooting on goal (A). The two players race for the puck (B). The player who gets the puck becomes the shooter and the player who does not get the puck becomes the back-checker. The puck carrier then tries to cut to the net while the back-checker tries to stop him (C).

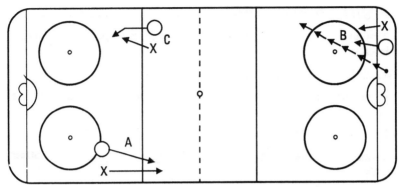

Figure 15-54

Penalty Killing and Power Play

All possible power play and penalty killing combinations should be practiced. The offensive aspect of penalty killing must also be practiced, as well as the defensive aspect of the power play.

Face-offs

All face-off positions and locations must be practiced.

Line Changes

Good coaches practice line changes so that the players can learn to make smooth line changes. The players must learn to get the puck into the other end for the change.

Broken Stick

The players must learn what to do when a teammate breaks a hockey stick and is temporarily out of the play.

Scrimmage

There are many scrimmage variations that can be used to emphasize certain points or patterns. The coach must learn to scrimmage according to the team's needs.

TIME LIMIT SCRIMMAGE

A player can only keep the puck for a certain number of seconds, 3, 4, 5, etc. This forces players to pass or make a play.

WHISTLE-DOWN SCRIMMAGE

The whistle is blown to stop play for every mistake or to emphasize a point.

NO RAISING THE PUCK SCRIMMAGE

At no time during the scrimmage is the puck to be raised off the ice.

MISTAKE SCRIMMAGE

Whenever a player makes a mistake, he is replaced by another player.

Pregame Warm-up

Each player carries a puck onto the ice, and stickhandles in a circle around the ice (diagram 15-55).

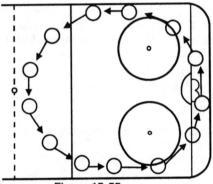

Figure 15-55

On command, the players stop, reverse directions and stickhandle around the ice in the opposite direction (diagram 15-56).

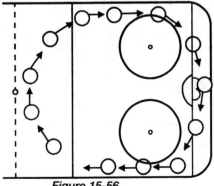

Figure 15-56

On command, the players join with a partner and make short passes to each other while skating around the rink (Figure 15-57).

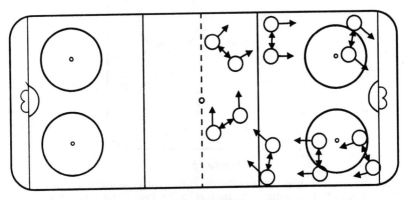

Figure 15-57

On command, the players line up for two-on-one rushes on one side of the ice and then switch to the other side (Figure 15-58).

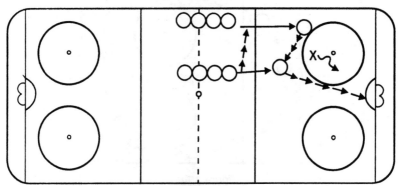

Figure 15-58

On command, the players line up with wingers in their wing positions and centerman at the center ice line. A defenseman passes the puck to the centerman, who in turn passes to one of his wings breaking to the net for a shot. The defenseman then passes to the same centerman who in turn pass to his other wing for a shot (Figure 15-59).

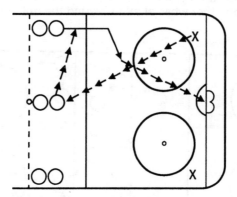

Figure 15-59

On command, the players skate backwards around the ice and then follow their captain off the ice to the bench or dressing room (Figure 15-60).

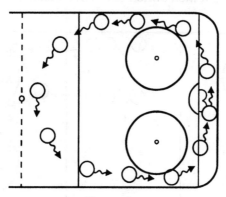

Figure 15-60

XVI. Glossary of Terms

ANGLE – the line deviating from straight on or 90 degrees.

    PLAYING THE ANGLE – when the goaltender positions himself to reduce the shooting area of an offen sive opponent.

    POOR ANGLE – shooting from an angle that is difficult to score from.

ATTACK – advancing the puck toward an opponent's goal.

ATTACKERS – the individuals advancing the puck toward an opponent's goal.

ATTACKING ZONE – the area of the rink from the opponent's blue line to the end of the rink that contains the opposition's goal.

BACK-CHECKING – checking an opponent from behind as they advance toward your goal.

BACKHAND – the action of shooting or passing in which the player's lower hand pulls the hockey stick to propel the puck.

BOARDS – the fence or wall that encloses the ice surface.

"BREAK AWAY" – when a player or group of players break towards the opposition's goal with the puck and no defenders between them and the goaltender.

BREAKOUT / BREAKOUT PLAY – when a team gains puck possession in their own end zone and and attempts to advance the puck into the neutral ice zone.

CENTER OF GRAVITY – the balance point of the athlete's body.

CHALK TALK – a talk or lecture in which diagrams are drawn on a blackboard or chalkboard to illustrate an idea or plan.

COGNITIVE – thinking, thought process.

COVERING THE MAN – similar to checking, being near the opponent and preventing him from attacking.

CUSTOM MADE – made to the user's exact specifications.

DEFENDER – a player guarding his own goal.

DEFENDING ZONE / DEFENSIVE END — a team's end zone where it tries to prevent goals from being scored.

DEKE, DEKING – fake moves designed to deceive an opponent.

DEFLECTION – redirecting the puck in another direction without stopping it.

FACE-OFF – the act of dropping the puck to the ice which begins play.

FAR WINGER / FAR DEFENSEMAN – the winger/defenseman farthest from the puck.

FOREHAND – the act of shooting or passing the puck where the lower hand pushes the hockey stick.

FORE-CHECKING – when the attacking team checks the opposition in the opponent's end zone. Fore-checking occurs when the opposition either has puck control or neither team has positive puck control.

FUNDAMENTALS – the basic skills of the game.

IMAGERY – when the mind visualizes a skill or performance.

INTERVAL TRAINING – a training method of alternating work and rest to a ratio.

LATERAL SKATING – skating or movement sideways in which the player's upper body remains facing forward.

LIE OF A HOCKEY STICK – the angle between the blade and shaft of the hockey stick.

MAN ADVANTAGE – a team with one more player on the ice than its opponent.

MAN-TO-MAN COVERAGE – when a player is assigned to check another player.

MBO (MANAGEMENT BY OBJECTIVES) – Setting goals to be accomplished by a certain date or within a time frame.

MECHANICS – the manipulation of the body to accomplish a skill.

NEAR WINGER/NEAR DEFENSEMAN — the winger/defenseman nearest the puck.

NEUTRAL ICE / NEUTRAL ZONE – the area between the two blue lines.

OFFENSE – controlling the puck or on the attack.

OFFENSIVE END – the end zone where the team attempts to score.

OPPOSITE WINGER – the winger farthest from the puck.

ORIENTATION – an awareness of one's surroundings in all directions.

PLAYING THE PERCENTAGE – performing to the most advantageous situation over time.

PENALTY KILLING – playing with one or two men less that the other team.

PIVOT – the action of turning while skating from forward to backward, or backward to forward.

POINT / POINTMAN – the defenseman in the attacking end zone.

POSITIONAL PLAY – where a player is supposed to be. One's position on the ice for the play or situation.

POWER PLAY – when a team that has a one- or two-man advantage.

PUCK CARRIER – the individual in control of the puck.

PUCK CONTROL – control of the puck in stickhandling, passing, pass receiving, shooting, tip-ins and rebounds.

REBOUNDS – when the puck bounces off the boards or a player. It usually refers to the shots that bounce off the goalie.

RINK – the walled area of ice where ice hockey is played.

RINK WIDE – a pass from one side of the ice to the other.

RUSH – advancing up the ice by a player(s).

SAFETY / SAFETY VALVE – the player positioned at the back of the play to help provided assistance if the designated play fails.

SCRAMBLES – a play with no pattern.

SCREEN – the action of blocking the view of someone, usually the goaltender.

SHORTHANDED – playing with fewer players than the other team.

STOCK ITEM – ready-made items.

SLOT / SLOTMAN – the area in front of the goal net and the player in that area.

STICKHANDLING – the skill of controlling the puck while moving or skating.

TIP-IN / TIP – deflecting a shot toward the goal.

TRAILER – the player skating behind, or following, the puck carrier.

VISUALIZATION – same as imagery.

WIDE – far to the side of an intended target.

ZEN – a philosophy of mind control.

ZONE COVERAGE – when a player covers or checks the players in his zone or area of responsibility.

The Spalding Youth League Series

Youth, Sports & Self Esteem
Darrell J. Burnett Ph.D.

Dr. Burnett, a clinical child psychologist, offers parents 12 specific guidelines for promoting their kids' self esteem through youth sports.

> 160 pages ● 5 1/4 x 8 1/4
> 0-940279-80-0 ● $12.95

Youth League Baseball
Skip Bertman

Each chapter of this book is devoted to a specific phase of the game. All the positions are covered, and position fundamentals are addressed.

> 192 pages ● 5 1/4 x 8 1/4
> 0-940279-68-1 ● $9.95

Youth League Football
Tom Flores & Bob O'Connor

Drills and coaching suggestions for all positions on the field, along with equipment information and hints for keeping the emphasis "play" rather than "work."

> 192 pages ● 5 1/4 x 8 1/4
> 0-940279-69-X ● $12.95

Youth League Soccer

A complete handbook for coaches that focuses on such important issues as conducting practice, inspiring young players, first-aid, and coaching during a game.

> 192 pages ● 5 1/4 x 8 1/4
> 0-940279-67-3 ● $9.95

Youth Tennis
Chuck Kriese

Featuring a unique three-level approach to athletic success, this book also includes an introduction to the rules and etiquette of the game.

> 160 pages ● 5 1/4 x 8 1/4
> 0-940279-88-6 ● $12.95

Youth Golf
Cliff Schrock

With instructional material from *Golf Digest, Youth Golf* is an outstanding golf handbook. Also features material on starting Hook A Kid on Golf golf leagues.

> 192 pages ● 5 1/4 x 8 1/4
> 0-940279-87-8 ● $12.95

Youth League Basketball
Joe Williams & Stan Wilson

Effective ways to teach basketball fundamentals that emphasize teamwork and unselfish play.

> 160 pages ● 5 1/4 x 8 1/4
> 0-940279-70-3 ● $12.95

All Masters Press titles, including those in the Youth League Series, are available in bookstores or by calling (800) 722-2677.